UNDERSTANDING AND LOVING A PERSON WITH

ALCOHOL OR DRUG ADDICTION

UNDERSTANDING AND LOVING A PERSON WITH

ALCOHOL OR DRUG ADDICTION

*Biblical and Practical Wisdom
to Build Empathy, Preserve Boundaries,
and Show Compassion*

STEPHEN ARTERBURN, M.Ed.
AND DAVID STOOP, Ph.D.

DAVID C COOK
transforming lives together

UNDERSTANDING AND LOVING A PERSON
WITH ALCOHOL OR DRUG ADDICTION
Published by David C Cook
4050 Lee Vance Drive
Colorado Springs, CO 80918 U.S.A.

Integrity Music Limited, a Division of David C Cook
Eastbourne, East Sussex BN23 6NT, England

The graphic circle C logo is a registered trademark of David C Cook.

The website addresses recommended throughout this book are offered as a
resource to you. These websites are not intended in any way to be or imply an
endorsement on the part of David C Cook, nor do we vouch for their content.

Details in some stories have been changed to protect
the identities of the persons involved.

Unless otherwise noted, all Scripture quotations are taken from the Holy
Bible, New Life Version. Copyright © 1969–2003 by Christian Literature
International, P.O. Box 777, Canby, OR 97013. Used by permission. Scripture
quotations marked NIV are taken from the Holy Bible, NEW INTERNATIONAL
VERSION®, NIV®. Copyright © 1973, 2011 by Biblica, Inc.® Used by permission.
All rights reserved worldwide. NEW INTERNATIONAL VERSION® and
NIV® are registered trademarks of Biblica, Inc. Use of either trademark for the
offering of goods or services requires the prior written consent of Biblica, Inc.
Scripture quotations marked NKJV are taken from the New King James Version®.
Copyright © 1982 by Thomas Nelson. Used by permission. All rights reserved.

LCCN 2017918222
ISBN 978-0-7814-1491-3
eISBN 978-0-8307-7222-3

© 2018 Stephen Arterburn
The Author is represented by and this book is published in association with the
literary agency of WordServe Literary Group, Ltd., www.wordserveliterary.com.

Cover Design: Amy Konyndyk

Printed in the United States of America
First Edition 2018

2 3 4 5 6 7 8 9 10 11

073018

Contents

Introduction

In 1978, I started working with alcoholics, went to my first AA meeting, and studied self-help programs of all kinds while attending seminary in Fort Worth, Texas. At the time, about 80 percent of all the Texans seeking treatment for addiction were dealing with an alcohol problem, and most had dealt with it for years before they sought help. Addiction to street drugs and prescription drugs comprised the other 20 percent. Since that time, the tables have completely turned. In many addiction treatment programs, most of the population is there with a problem with prescription drugs, and often they only turn to street drugs when they become the cheaper option. Most likely, the person you love has a problem with prescription or street drugs.

There is another glaring problem that does not quite fall under the category of addiction. It revolves around the legalization of marijuana. The battle cry of the movement is that marijuana is not addictive and is less harmful than alcohol. But more often than not, there are complications alongside marijuana use. Living at home in the room where you grew up because you are not motivated to work is a common problem. I frequently receive calls from parents whose children have had a very bad trip from LSD or mushrooms and ended up in the emergency room. No, their child isn't addicted, but he or she is dependent on a chemical that is causing great difficulty and struggle. Those children need to secure independence from a chemical just like those hard-drinking

Texans needed to get help to stop consuming beer after doing so habitually for fifty years.

The fact that you have picked up this book indicates that there is a very good chance that someone you care about deeply is struggling with alcohol, prescription drugs, street drugs, marijuana, or a combination of two or more of these chemicals. I know this book will help you understand that person and his or her problem. But more than that, I am hoping that you learn what to do to help your loved one and develop the courage to do what you need to do. If not, the problem will get worse, the misery will intensify, and the consequences of your choices and the choices of the one you love will continue to have increasingly destructive impacts. I don't want that for you or anyone else, so I am extremely grateful that you have found this book. Here is why.

More than thirty years ago, I presented a seminar at my church in Newport Beach, California, titled "That Christian Next to You May Be an Alcoholic." To my surprise, Dr. Dave Stoop and his wife, Dr. Jan Stoop, attended, and it began a friendship that remains stronger today than ever. They had attended the seminar because of a family member who was struggling with a drug problem. And all these years later, that wonderful family member is clean and sober and deeply connected with the family.

Because of this experience, no one is better qualified to speak and write on the subject of understanding, helping, loving, and supporting someone with a problem with chemical dependency. Dave knows so much about so many things, but this problem hit home, and Dave and Jan did what needed to be done to help the one they loved. It was not easy, and it was not instant, but it was effective. Now for the first time, Dave has brought all that he learned and all that he experienced to those who can benefit from it the most. I am so proud to be Dave's friend and coauthor on so many books that have helped millions, and I am so proud of this amazing book that comes directly from Dave's heart. What you will find here is not a guarantee that the one you love will get better, but it is a path and a process that will lead you to your best hope.

—Stephen Arterburn

CHAPTER ONE

You Are Not Alone

It was a story I'd heard many times over the years, but it felt like it could have been my own story.

When Ron and Jenny had called, they were desperate for an appointment. When they sat down in my office, they poured out their pain and concerns. Trouble had hit their family, and they didn't know what to do about it. No one else in their circle of friends seemed to know what to do either. They had always believed that drug addiction was something that was only supposed to show up in families with major problems—not in their family.

Ron had gone back to school to be a therapist, but he hadn't taken the one course on addiction and alcoholism yet. I remembered that when I was in my doctoral program preparing to be a psychologist, there weren't *any* courses offered on either alcoholism or drug addiction.

When one of Ron and Jenny's daughters started withdrawing from the family, they attributed it to her possibly having ADHD or some adolescent issue or disorder, but they never thought it could be an addiction. I often meet with people who are convinced the problem with their child or spouse is really depression or bipolar disorder. Maybe he's gotten caught up in the wrong crowd or recently experienced a traumatic event. Anything but an addiction.

Everyone begins the healing process by facing the truth. But often, when we are confronted with the fact that someone is addicted, we still want to focus on things besides the addiction— like how her use of substances was just a way to "self-medicate." Parents may feel that if they can solve the obvious problem of why their child needs to self-medicate, her addiction will just go away.

So Ron and Jenny were there to seek help in finding the cause of the problem as they saw it: a change in their daughter's attitude toward the family. She was seldom home, and when she was, she stayed in her room with the door closed. She had also stopped talking to everyone in the family, including her brothers. Her attitude toward school had changed as well: her grades were falling, and eventually, she'd started cutting classes. The typical school system often can't help because it's already overloaded with its own problems—problems we as parents also often blame for our kids' issues at school. On top of all that, Ron and Jenny were concerned about the kinds of friends their daughter was starting to hang around with. But when they tried to deal with any of these issues, their daughter became angry and defensive. Ron and Jenny's own heated response led to everyone getting more and more frustrated.

They didn't know until later that one of their daughter's "friends" had introduced her to heroin on her sixteenth birthday. From that point on, for six years, they said it felt like the family was living in hell. School soon stopped being an issue because their daughter had simply dropped out. She came home only to sleep—meals were not on the agenda anymore. Holidays and celebratory events were times of extreme tension. She would disappear completely at times, only to show up again when she needed something.

Ron and Jenny had just described to me what are, unfortunately, common experiences for parents of a kid addicted to drugs. My own family's story is similar to that of Ron and Jenny's. One member of my family entered thirteen different treatment programs over his years of addiction. He left many after a day or two, as they were ineffective programs that only tried to shame the addict further. In one, he had to wear a toilet seat around his neck at the beginning, but they didn't seem to know what to do with him after that. He did complete several programs, and twice, we went through what was called "family week." Those weeks were enlightening, but I guess we just didn't get the message that we were part of the problem, so both times, it wasn't long before he relapsed and disappeared again.

Finally, our friend Stephen Arterburn, who had walked with us through most of our struggle, recommended a program developed by Joe Pursch. Dr. Pursch is the medical doctor who successfully treated Billy Carter and Betty Ford for their alcoholism. It was a totally family-focused treatment program, and everyone in our family had to be involved.

My wife, Jan, and I were in a group with other addicts/alcoholics, and our family members were in a different group with other parents and addicts/alcoholics. I was licensed as a psychologist and was not used to being in a group—I typically *ran* groups. So it was awkward, and I remember introducing myself and then adding,

"I'm here because one of our kids has a problem." Sitting opposite me was a twenty-year-old who I learned later was an alcoholic. He almost came off his chair as he said to me, "That's what my dad said when he first came here. You're going to find out you're here because *you* have a problem!" And I eventually realized that he was correct!

Two things I experienced through that program changed everything. First, we had to attend weekly Alcoholics Anonymous (AA) speaker meetings, and it was the best education I have ever experienced regarding addiction. We attended these meetings almost thirty years ago, but some of the speakers were so helpful that I still remember the things they said. A *speaker meeting* is an AA meeting where you come in, sit down, listen as someone shares their story of addiction, and then get up and leave without saying anything yourself. I learned more from those meetings than from any continuing education course on addiction I have taken.

The second thing we had to do was attend group sessions, family counseling sessions, and Al-Anon meetings. Al-Anon meetings are for those who are living with an alcoholic or addict, while AA meetings are primarily for the acting alcoholic and NA meetings (Narcotics Anonymous) are specifically for drug addicts. In our weekly Al-Anon meetings, it was a different kind of eye-opening experience. At first, we thought the parents of the addicts and alcoholics in the meetings didn't care about their kids, because they seemed to have lives of their own—they knew how to laugh and enjoy themselves. But as we continued to attend, we learned that they cared deeply—they had just released themselves of the responsibility to change their sons or daughters.

Over the years before this, I had twice tried to set up a miraculous healing experience for our kid. Both times, it seemed God was busy somewhere else—perhaps with your child. Eventually, I would get over my frustration with God while still praying for that miracle daily. When our miracle finally came, more than twenty-eight years ago, I had nothing to do with it—God gets all the credit and glory. It taught me the lesson about being powerless in a way I would never forget.

Walt

Walt was my wife's distant relative, whom she had known since he was just a little boy. Jan remembers when a car hit Walt, at the age of six; from then on, he walked with a major limp and had chronic pain. When he became an adult, he took over the responsibility for his pain medications. The meds would help at first, but eventually, he'd become tolerant to the dosage, and the doctor would have to either increase the strength of the pills or change the medication.

When his doctor tried to get him to stop taking the meds, he developed a network of several doctors to prescribe the pills for him. In this way, he was able to get enough of the pain meds he had become dependent on and thought he needed. No one knew he was doing this, not even the doctors.

When he died of an overdose some years ago, my family gathered his belongings, since he was living in our area and had no other relatives close by. We were not prepared for what we found when we opened one of his cupboards: bottle after bottle of pain killers—too many to count. He was a casualty of a different kind of drug addiction and the victim of its consequences long before prescription drug addiction became the widespread problem it is today.

Addiction to prescription meds has been called "the hidden epidemic" because it can easily go unnoticed. No one knew that Walt was addicted; it was his secret. Things have changed somewhat today, as doctors and pharmacists now have methods that will alert them to suspicious use of a medication, making an addiction harder to hide. But at the same time, addicts are increasingly turning to illegal drugs to supplement their prescribed medications.

Marty

Marty was an integral part of her boss's business. Together, they ran a smooth, successful operation. She knew her boss was a recovering alcoholic, but since it was under control, Marty didn't even think about it—that is, until Robert relapsed. At first, she was not aware of the impending problem. She didn't know he had started drinking some wine with his dinner. Even when he started working from home, using his cell phone to keep Marty informed, she wasn't worried.

But when Robert stopped answering the phone, Marty knew that was different. She wondered if he had fallen or somehow injured himself. Out of concern, she went to his house to check on him. He was alive, and there was no evidence of an accident. Marty instead found eleven empty wine bottles on the kitchen counter and more in the trash can outside. She questioned him, and of course, he made light of it all. When she found out he hadn't eaten in several days, she made him dinner.

Marty was concerned about not just her job but also Robert's health. She knew that she could manage the business for some time, but in the long run, Robert was essential to its success. So she decided that, every other day, she would either fix him dinner or bring him takeout. Then she started to worry about him driving to the store in order to replenish his stock of wine, and so she offered to go to the store to buy it for him. She shared her concerns with him, and he listened sympathetically, but nothing changed.

When a friend of Marty's found out what she was doing, she strongly suggested that Marty start coming with her to Al-Anon meetings. Because Marty's friend had started to face her own issues, she knew an enabler when she saw one. Gradually, Marty started to understand that she was helping Robert perpetuate his alcohol problem. She was doing all kinds of things for him that only freed him to continue his addiction.

Finally, she not only stopped helping Robert but also told him she was going to look for another job. She was done! It didn't take Robert long to call a recovering friend, one whom he had been avoiding, and ask him for a ride to the hospital for treatment. Marty had needed to learn that she too had a problem! She was an enabler, and she dealt with it!

Chemical Addictions

Addictions to drugs—legal prescription drugs, illegal drugs, or alcohol—are examples of what's referred to as a chemical addiction. A chemical is ingested into the body, and the body reacts. A person becomes dependent on the chemical, sometimes very quickly.

The addictive process starts as soon as the chemical enters the body. Some drugs take time for dependency to develop. Other drugs are almost instantly addictive once ingested—for example, if one hundred people were given a dose of heroin, which is highly addictive, ninety-nine of them would become addicted to heroin with just one dose. So anyone can become addicted—it is no respecter of persons!

Alcohol is different. Not everyone can become addicted to alcohol. Studies estimate that 8 to 10 percent of people who drink alcohol can become alcoholics. The majority of people can't become addicted because they cannot ingest enough alcohol to become addicted. They may get very sleepy after drinking one or two drinks or experience a blinding headache if they have more than one. Some literally get sick if they drink any alcohol. These are examples of people who cannot ingest enough alcohol to become dependent and addicted.

When alcoholism runs in the extended biological family, it's possible that random offspring will be born with the alcohol receptors already in their genes, waiting for that first drink. If they drink one drink, they will become chemically dependent on alcohol and be alcoholics. For the 8 to 10 percent who are born with these alcohol receptors, when they start drinking, they will also have a high tolerance for alcohol. They can drink a twenty-four pack of beer in a day and show no signs of having drank that much. They were the ones who others admired in college because they were able to "hold their liquor," but they are also the ones who will become alcoholics. They have to be able to ingest enough alcohol at any given period of time to become addicted.

An alcoholic is in real danger when they stop drinking. They face alcohol withdrawal, which can be life-threatening. But in the early stages of their dependency, no matter how much they drink, they seldom, if ever, get drunk. Unfortunately, this gives them and their family members a false sense of security that they won't have a problem.

Most people define the typical alcoholic as the drunkard on skid row. However, when you look at that person, you are seeing the final stages of the disease of alcoholism. Alcoholics end up on skid row after years of abuse—after they have lost their families and their jobs and have no means to support their former lifestyles.

Some people addicted to alcohol say that they can't be alcoholic because they only drink beer. That's a myth. One twelve-ounce can of beer has the same amount of alcohol as a five-ounce glass of wine or a shot and a half of hard liquor. It's the alcohol, not the conveyor of the alcohol, that counts.

There is also what is called a "problem drinker." This is someone who abuses alcohol but wouldn't be considered dependent on it. A problem drinker typically drinks to excess in order to get drunk or to numb himself to some life trauma. He doesn't meet the criteria for having an addiction in that he does not experience the same issues as someone who is addicted, aside from a nasty hangover. But living with a problem drinker is about the same as living with an active alcoholic. If you have a problem drinker in the family, your task is the same: don't argue about the problem, just get help and support for yourself.

Process Addictions

Process addictions are different but have the same negative consequences as chemical addictions. Here the person does not ingest anything, but she becomes addicted to the "high" she experiences when engaged in a particular behavior.

The *high* is a rush of hormones in the brain. They are usually pleasure hormones, at least at first: hormones such as dopamine, oxytocin, and even adrenaline. Like with chemical addictions, you can build up a tolerance to them, so a person addicted to some behavioral process needs to intensify the experience to get the same high. He continues this search for that high in spite of the negative consequences he increasingly experiences, such as overwhelming feelings of guilt, shame, or remorse, as well as the negative consequences of his actions.

Process addictions include sex addiction, food addiction, gambling addiction, video game addiction, and work or spending addictions, along with other compulsive behaviors. There are four reasons these are considered addictions:

1. The person with the addiction struggles with trying to stop or gain control over the behavior. Various types of strategies are developed, and all of them eventually fail. Her willpower is just not powerful enough.
2. The behavior causes problems in the person with the addiction's significant relationships. Other people feel frustrated and/or betrayed by the addictive behavior.
3. The person with the addiction experiences negative consequences that are directly caused by her inability to stop the

addictive behavior. In spite of becoming obese, bankrupt, or unfaithful, her behavior continues. We'll see this in the examples that follow.

4. In spite of all of this, the person with the addiction cannot stop engaging in the addictive behavior. She's tried, and she continues to try, but all to no avail!

Thomas

Thomas was the pastor of a small rural church, if any place in Southern California could be called "rural." The church hired him full time and already had a secretary who was part time in the mornings only. It was not a good situation for him, but at first, that was his secret alone.

Thomas was a sex addict. He had been watching porn since he was eleven years old, when an older brother had introduced him to *Playboy* magazine.

As Thomas continued to feed his addiction, what once was satisfying became borderline boring. So in his afternoons alone in the church office, he began to explore other sites. Eventually, he got involved in a sexual chat room and started having conversations with a woman. It didn't take long for their conversations to escalate, and she began to call him on his office phone—that way, there was no record that he had initiated the call.

The more they talked, the more they wanted to talk, and then they started talking about him coming out to meet her. When they eventually scheduled a time, Thomas couldn't buy the airline ticket, so the woman paid for it. Thomas told his wife he had been talking to a church in the Midwest and that they were flying him out for an interview. He even told her what church it was and in what city, thinking that she would never check it out.

However, the third time he went for an "interview," his wife became suspicious. She remembered the name of the church and looked it up on the Internet, then called the number she found, asking for her husband. They had never heard of him, and they had no interviews scheduled.

Now she was concerned. Thomas had left his computer in the church office, so his wife went to the church to check it for clues. She had no idea what he had been doing and was sickened by what she found in his history. She sat there stunned, and then she called the church's chairman of the board and asked him to come to the office.

Together, in their disbelief, they started to develop a plan of action. He would go with her to pick Thomas up at the airport so he could do the confronting. They also figured they had to find out what he was doing on his trips first, though it was hard not to imagine what was going on. Once they knew what they were dealing with, they would flesh out the plan with the help of a local therapist.

Of course, Thomas was shocked to see the chairman of the board when his wife came to pick him up at the airport. At first, Thomas was defensive and stuck to his story that he had been meeting with a church, but the evidence was stacked against him. He finally confessed what he had been doing and agreed to follow a plan of action.

But within a week, Thomas decided he was finished. He resigned from the church, told his wife he wanted a divorce, left her and his children, and moved to a different state to be with his chat-room love. After all, she was what could be called "porn-friendly." That's how powerful his process addiction was!

Andy

Andy's story is a little different, although it starts out the same. Andy was introduced to pornography when he was thirteen. A few of his buddies knew he was looking at porn; they had introduced each other to the websites, carefully choosing who to let into their ranks. They had to be careful because they were all active in their church's youth group. All along, Andy felt guilty about his involvement with porn, but he had convinced himself that the problem would go away once he was older and got married.

When he married, his time spent looking at porn decreased at first, but when he started leaving home on business trips, he made up for lost time. His obsession with porn was still there.

About five years into his marriage, his wife caught him, and they had a "truth session." His wife felt betrayed—and rightly so—but they talked it through and agreed to go to counseling together. It felt like they were on the right track. They spent a year in counseling together and worked on a number of issues as well as Andy's pornography use.

Ten years later, on a business trip, something triggered in him the "curiosity" to check out a porn site he had heard about. Before he realized it, five hours had elapsed—he had been totally lost in what he was watching. He thought it was a one-time "slip," but soon, he found he was watching porn as frequently as he had in his teen years.

A couple of months later, his wife caught him again, and this time, the response wasn't couples counseling; it was what they should have done ten years earlier—an *Every Man's Battle* workshop. The workshop is held by one of the New Life Ministries, and it's an intensive weekend that has successfully helped men overcome their addiction to pornography. *Every Man's Battle* helped Andy learn, among other things, how to set up a network of continuous accountability with other men. Now, five years later, he and his wife have a marriage that has been restored!

Owning Mahowny

Some years ago, while I was teaching a class on addiction at Fuller Theological Seminary, we began talking about gambling. Someone suggested we watch the movie *Owning Mahowny*, which is based on the true story of Brian Malony.

In the film, set in 1982, Dan Mahowny is promoted to assistant branch manager of a Canadian bank in Toronto and given access to large accounts. He gradually starts skimming money from fake loans to finance his trips to Atlantic City casinos. Soon, he is making weekly trips, and the casino managers are treating him like a king, flying him from Toronto to Atlantic City and back in their private plane. Eventually, he embezzles more than $10 million from the bank to pay his losses from gambling both with bookies and in casinos.

Just as the Canadian authorities are about to arrest him, he makes one last trip to Atlantic City. In a scene I'll never forget, he is shown playing blackjack in a private room. He is winning and has accumulated a massive amount of money. A casino worker who knows his pending problem with the law back home begs him to stop while he is ahead, but Mahowny refuses to listen. He continues to gamble until he has lost it all.

When he returns home, the authorities are waiting for him. He pleads guilty to fraud and spends six years in prison. After his release, he stops gambling, marries, and has three sons. The Canadian bank pursues court action against the Atlantic City casinos and settles for an undisclosed sum. The court also requires all Atlantic City casinos to close for a whole day as part of the settlement.

People who are addicted to gambling often end up bankrupt, facing foreclosures and other financial, legal, and personal consequences. One of the most powerful reward systems is the random kind that we feed when gambling. That's what can keep you coming back for more, even though you know that in the end, you will lose. That is what makes gambling addictive, and anyone who has gambled can experience it.

Nick

Nick is a twenty-nine-year-old who lives in the basement of his parents' house. He has created a comfortable room for himself there, and he only emerges to eat, preferably when the rest of the family is asleep. He stays up most of the night playing video games, sometimes alone, and sometimes with people he only knows through the games.

Addiction to fantasy video games is a growing phenomenon. The graphics are improving, becoming more realistic. There are always new games being introduced, and the ability to connect via headset with other players can be fascinating. Add to that the ability to take on a fictional character's identity and live life in an alternate reality, and it can become very addictive.

That's what has happened to Nick. He leaves his virtual world to work about ten hours a week. That gives him enough money for food and gas. The rest of the time he spends sleeping during the day and playing games at night. His only "friends" are the unnamed players he plays certain games with. No need for college or future goals—the biggest dream he has is to create a game someday, but he never considers how he would do that.

He's addicted, and the evidence is in his inability to connect with others in person, his lack of ambition, and his very unhealthy lifestyle. Fortunately, only one in ten who play video games end up becoming addicted.

Other Process Addictions

There are also those who spend too much, work or eat compulsively, or live out any other compulsive type of behavior that is out of their control. While process addictions may not make someone dependent on ingested chemicals, they still create physical dependence. The brain releases certain hormones when a person experiences a "high" during the activity, so a person can become addicted to the adrenaline rush he gets or the satisfied feeling that comes with the release of oxytocin in the brain.

What turns these activities into an addiction is that the person continues the behavior in spite of its negative impact. Another sign of an addiction is the anger expressed by the person when her access to her chosen addiction is threatened in some way—she may get ready for a fight if someone even mentions that the behavior could be a problem. This may lead the person who loves the addict to back away and say to himself that maybe it isn't an addiction. Maybe his loved one is just depressed or under a lot of stress, or perhaps her self-esteem is in the pits. Many times, enablers would rather deal with those issues than confront the actual problem: the addiction itself.

While stress, depression, or low self-esteem may all be factors, the focus of any addiction treatment must always begin with the addictive behavior. Until that has been dealt with, focusing on the other problems will derail treatment. The addiction must always be the priority. Every situation we've described in this chapter is treatable. There is hope for healing. But before we look at treatment, let's put your loved one's problem in perspective.

CHAPTER TWO

Just the Facts, Ma'am

If you want to be a genuine agent of healing and change, you must know what you're up against. It's easy to think you are helping the person when, in reality, without realizing it, you are actually only helping him continue to engage in the problematic behavior. That's why it is called "enabling."

It isn't an easy lesson to learn; I know from experience. When I was a young associate pastor, my understanding of alcoholism was reflective of what most churches believed at that time—that alcoholism was a sin, so if someone accepted Christ's atonement for their sin, then their alcoholism would no longer be a problem. I believed that, and I was serving in a church that believed that. I also had not had any experience with—or even awareness of—the existence of alcoholism as a problem apart from the stereotypical kind found on skid row. I had grown up oblivious to its reality. But that was about to change.

It was common knowledge that the father of a young family in our church had a "drinking problem." He seldom came to church with his family, perhaps in part because he knew he was the subject of a lot of concern and a lot of prayer. But he occasionally came to a Sunday-night service, and one Sunday night, when the invitation was given, he came forward and confessed to his "sin of drinking." It appeared to those around the altar that after much prayer for him, and now over him, he had finally entered the kingdom, and therefore his alcohol problem was "solved."

About a month later, he was back at the altar, for he had sinned and drank again. He was desperate to solve the problem, and he wept as he confessed. This happened twice more, and then things seemed to settle down.

As the associate pastor, I was given the task of keeping track of the family, making sure they were in church together, and seeing if they had any needs. They came faithfully for about five or six months, and then I gradually moved on to other tasks. It was some time later that I noticed they had stopped coming. I called them on the phone, and the wife answered. I asked how they were doing, and as we talked, I said that we had missed them at the church. "Oh," she said, "we were doing so well after the last time, but then the alcohol problem came back. We felt like we had failed, and eventually, we just stopped coming."

I was surprised—that wasn't supposed to happen. She could tell by my silence that I was concerned, so she went on: "My husband finally went to AA—something he had avoided for years—and it's working. He hasn't had a drink in over a year! And I've been going to Al-Anon for myself, and that has really made a difference in our family."

I think I just wished them well—because I really didn't know what to say—then said we would continue to pray for them and hung up. To say I was confused was an understatement. The story didn't fit into my belief system.

However, over the years, my understanding of alcoholism and addiction grew. Some years later, at another church, I got to know Stephen Arterburn and had him teach a class that we called "That Christian Sitting Next to You Could Be an Alcoholic." As the class progressed, we didn't realize it, but we had opened Pandora's box.

One of the things Steve taught was that when you look around your church some Sunday morning, or at any gathering of people, know that one out of every three people there has been touched in some way by alcoholism, and one out of ten is probably an alcoholic (that statistic has since been updated to one in thirteen). The point is that being a Christian doesn't exempt anyone from the possibility of addiction.

Alcoholism: Sin or Disease?

To understand addiction and alcoholism, I had to resolve the sin question. That question has been a battleground since 1804, when Thomas Trotter, a Scottish physician, wrote an article in which he stated that what was called "drunkenness" was a disease produced by remote causes and led to disorders in the person's health. This sparked a controversy that is still being debated in some circles.

For years, both the church and the medical profession opposed Trotter's views. For the church, it seemed that if it was a disease, it absolved the alcoholic from any responsibility for his or her actions; for the medical profession, it meant they were responsible for treating something they saw as simply the alcoholic's lack of motivation to stop. Though both the church and the medical profession have come to a better understanding of the nature of alcoholism since then, there are still those who continue to espouse these arguments.

I believe that addictions and alcoholism are diseases that must be treated. I also believe that addicts and alcoholics are responsible for a large number of sins. But treatments that only see sin as the issue are mostly weak and unsuccessful. Effective treatments have been developed by working from the point of view that addiction and alcoholism are diseases—physical problems that, if untreated, will progress to the point of causing a person to deteriorate and eventually die.

What I started to discover as a young pastor was that the disease model allows for treatment, whereas the sin model did little to help us understand the nature of alcoholism and thus combat it. When we define alcoholism, as I once did, as the "bum on skid row," we are defining alcoholism only by its end result. In the earlier stages, the alcoholic is seldom drunk and, for the most part, manages his life despite his drinking.

The Bible condemns drunkenness. Ephesians 5:18 tells us, "Don't be drunk with wine, because that will ruin your life." Since the alcoholic seldom gets drunk in the early stages, he thinks he's off the hook. But the truth is, alcoholics do get drunk—but it's when they stop drinking. If they sit in the bar for a short time after their last drinks, they run the risk of getting a DUI, because when their blood alcohol level begins to drop, they run into trouble, such as accidents and tickets.

As I got to know the young man who first confronted me in the initial group therapy meeting for my family member, I found out that he considered himself an alcoholic even though he was only twenty years old. He told me he could pass the highway patrol's sobriety test even when he had a blood alcohol level of .28, as he had the last time. He could also pass the sobriety test even when his dad administered it to him, which his dad had to do quite often. For nonalcoholics, having a blood alcohol level that high would put them in a coma. The legal limit for driving while intoxicated in the United States is .08; his level was three and a half times that, and he could still function normally.

He was young. He wasn't on skid row. But he was an alcoholic in the early stages of the disease. He called himself an alcoholic because of what he had learned about himself in his treatment program, and his self-diagnosis was in part because of his high tolerance. A high tolerance for alcohol is the primary criteria for someone to be considered an alcoholic. That means the person you went to college with who could drink everyone else under the table and not show any sign of being drunk is probably an alcoholic today, because he could drink enough alcohol to literally become addicted to it. These people are born with a liver malfunction that allows them to build up dangerous enzymes in their systems during the body's processing of alcohol that don't seem to harm them. Alcoholics also have receptors in the cells of their bodies that, once triggered, will cause them to actually crave alcohol.

One of the treatment doctors I've met gives this test to those who think they may be alcoholics: Go out, buy a six-pack of beer, and put it in the refrigerator. Eliminate all other alcoholic drinks from the house. If the six-pack of beer is still there after thirty days, this doctor believes you aren't an alcoholic.

The test is based on the alcoholic's natural craving for alcohol. Your loved one may not be a big beer drinker, or she may prefer wine or hard liquor, but it's still alcohol, and if there is no other alcohol available, she can't leave the six-pack there. She will drink it all. A person who drinks but leaves the six-pack there probably isn't dealing with an actual craving for alcohol.

Those without this high tolerance get drunk after several drinks, fall asleep, or literally get sick and throw up. From the beginning, they can't drink enough to develop an actual addiction. But anyone can build up a tolerance for alcohol over time, so problem drinkers who gradually build up their intake of alcohol can eventually become addicted. They may not have been born with the propensity to be alcoholics, but they have worked their way up to the diagnosis.

We also say the alcoholic is "born with" the potential to abuse alcohol based on another determining factor: heredity. It is believed that alcoholism is a generational issue that is based on not just behavior but physical inheritance. It's not passed on to everyone but dispersed randomly among siblings and generations. So both tolerance and heredity, along with increasing problems with relationships, are the signs of an alcoholic.

One of the things I was taught was that when you wonder how many drinks the person you love has had, ask them. We all have a tendency to minimize how much, so if it's a man you are asking, double what he says. But if it's a woman you are asking, you need to multiply it by four. Female alcoholics tend to stay in the shadows more, often only drinking at home. Treatment is complicated because they need to care for their children, and they often can't do a thirty-day treatment program because they have no answer to the question of who will take care of the kids.

Since addiction is a progressive disease, it means that eventually the addict/alcoholic you love will reach the condition described in Proverbs 23:29–35:

> *Who has anguish? Who has sorrow?*
>> *Who is always fighting? Who is always complaining?*
>> *Who has unnecessary bruises? Who has bloodshot eyes?*
> *It is the one who spends long hours in the taverns,*
>> *trying out new drinks.*
> *Don't gaze at the wine, seeing how red it is,*
>> *how it sparkles in the cup, how smoothly it goes down.*
> *For in the end it bites like a poisonous snake;*
>> *it stings like a viper.*
> *You will see hallucinations,*
>> *and you will say crazy things.*
> *You will stagger like a sailor tossed at sea,*
>> *clinging to a swaying mast.*
> *And you will say, "They hit me, but I didn't feel it.*
>> *I didn't even know it when they beat me up.*
> *When will I wake up*
>> *so I can look for another drink?"*

… and by the time that describes a person, skid row isn't far behind. That's the Bible's description of addicts/alcoholics. They are preoccupied with their addiction. They see hallucinations, they say stupid things, they get hit and don't feel it, and when they wake up, all they can think about is that they need another drink!

The fact that alcoholism is a disease gives hope for treatment. But it doesn't eliminate the fact that many of the behaviors of the alcoholic are sinful. As a disease, it causes people to act in increasingly sinful ways, as do all addictions.

We pay a high price as a country for alcoholism. The Centers for Disease Control and Prevention says that alcohol abuse accounts for eighty-eight thousand deaths each year, making it the fourth leading preventable cause of death in the United States. In each year alone, more than four million emergency room visits and almost two million hospitalizations are related to alcohol abuse. In addition, 41 percent of fatal traffic accidents are related to alcohol, and about 20 percent of suicide victims are alcoholics. It's a costly and deadly addiction!

Marijuana

Although there is a segment of the population who would disagree, marijuana has become one of the most abused drugs in our country. Even though there is an ever-growing gap between what researchers are finding and the myths surrounding its use, that various states have legalized its use for "recreational" purposes has intensified the controversy.

Some people argue that since it is legal in some states, it must be safe and harmless. Or they argue that since it is a "natural" plant, it must be harmless. The truth is that there are more than four hundred different chemicals in marijuana, and they all affect a person in some way. The chief chemical, and the one that causes intoxication, is THC (short for tetrahydrocannabinol). It's a proven fact that any substance that causes intoxication creates changes in the person, both physically and mentally. This is also the chemical that creates dependency and addiction.

People smoke marijuana in hand-rolled cigarettes called "joints" or in either a dry pipe or a water pipe called a "bong." They can also hollow out a cigar and refill it with marijuana, creating what is called a "blunt." Sometimes the abuser will add more powerful drugs to the marijuana, such as crack cocaine or PCP. For those who want to avoid smoking, a "vaporizer" evaporates the drug and lets them inhale the vapors instead.

To get a greater level of intoxication, a relatively new method involves smoking THC-rich resins, known as "hash oil," "honey oil," "wax," "budder," or "shatter," depending on the result desired. The abuser will have to use lighter fluid to make the resin, a process that can be just as hazardous as the use of the resin.

The consequences of marijuana use are denied by many, including the media. But typical abusers may try to hold the smoke in their lungs as long as they can in order to increase the effect. When they do this, smoking one joint gives as much exposure to cancer as smoking four to five cigarettes.

Long-term use of marijuana has been found to affect brain development. Users under the age of twenty-five (which is when the brain is fully developed) can reduce their ability to think, to remember, and to learn because marijuana affects the neural connections within the brain. These effects can last a long time and may even be permanent. It can also lower a person's IQ score significantly. Marijuana affects the prefrontal cortex, which is the executive part of our brains. It affects the parts of the brain that manage coordination, vision, and movement, as well as the seat of our emotions—the limbic system. It's also the part of the brain that makes judgments and decisions, and it's where motivation is centered. Low motivation is a major effect in those who are frequent users.

The big argument, though, is whether or not marijuana is addictive. Those who abuse marijuana, especially before age eighteen, are especially vulnerable to becoming addicted—they can't stop using the drug even though they experience negative consequences due to dependence on it.

Andy is a recovering alcoholic who was frustrated about the slow process of change in his life. One day, his sponsor found out why—he had been smoking pot with a girlfriend. His sponsor gave him this advice: "Ninety meetings in ninety days!" He broke up with his girlfriend and started attending a meeting every day. His alcohol recovery got back on track, he was motivated, he got a better job, and he started socializing more with others after the meetings.

He continued going to meetings frequently after doing his ninety meetings, and it seemed like he had his life back on track. Then he got back together with his girlfriend. AA meetings became optional, his hours at work were cut back, and he stopped talking with his sponsor. He was back on pot and had all the myths about its use memorized. When a recovery buddy confronted him, he had all the answers and even announced that he was looking into moving to Colorado, where recreational pot is legal.

What about Medical Marijuana?

So far, the US Food and Drug Administration (FDA) has not approved, or even recognized, the medical use of marijuana. However, studies of one of the chemicals in marijuana—a cannabinoid called "cannabidiol" (CBD)—have convinced the FDA to approve some medications that contain CBD, since it does not affect the mind or behavior and it has been found to be effective in reducing pain and inflammation. Some scientists have been working at breeding marijuana plants that are low in THC—the intoxicant—and high in cannabinoids.

Illegal Drugs and Prescription Drugs

Several years ago, before the opioid epidemic hit the country, I was speaking at an event sponsored by a treatment center in Florida. In a conversation with the medical director of the program, he offhandedly said that in the "old days," they treated mostly alcoholics, but now, at least 70 percent of their inpatients at any time were there because of a prescription drug addiction. He then went on to describe what legal meds they were addicted to.

I was surprised by some of the prescription drugs people were addicted to. I knew that Valium, Xanax, Ativan, and Klonopin were highly addictive. But he included Adderall and Ritalin on his list. I knew that college students would often start taking Adderall or Ritalin in order to stay alert so they could stay up all night studying for their exams or for some other less important reason. But they are often unaware of the risk of addiction—as was I. I've since worked with people who started abusing Adderall in college in order to stay awake and ended up addicted. Some of them told me they actually ingested the drug by grinding it into a powder and snorting it.

What has been called the "opioid addiction epidemic"—even by the US Department of Health and Human Services—is now seen as the prime example of prescription drug addiction. The National Institutes of Health (NIH) estimates that fifty-four million of us in the United States have used opioid medications for nonmedical reasons. Nonmedical reasons include taking someone else's prescription or simply taking the medication in order to feel good or even normal. Of those who use medication for nonmedical purposes, 54 percent are women and about 30 percent are adolescents. One man says he takes opioids because without them, he is extremely uncomfortable in his own skin. He needs the opioid just to feel normal. The NIH estimates that at least 12 percent of those who think they are safe from this epidemic will end up being addicted. That's a lot of people!

The Opioid Epidemic

Anyone who takes prescription opioids can become addicted to them, and once addicted, it is very hard to stop. My wife, Jan, recently had one of her knees replaced. I know how painful it is, for I had one of mine replaced several years ago. And even the surgeon must know how painful it is because he prescribed one hundred oxycodone pills (Percocet) with instructions to take one every four to six hours as needed.

Jan did as she was told for the first nine days, and then one night, she missed a dose and then delayed taking one in the morning. It wasn't long before the pain increased, but she also started to feel like she was shaking on the inside. She said it was a weird feeling. The physical therapist who came to the house that same morning told her she was experiencing withdrawal and then explained that Percocet is one of the strongest of the addictive opioids. She suggested that Jan switch to something in the midrange, like tramadol. Tramadol is a less powerful synthetic opioid, though it is just as addictive as any other opioid. Jan called her doctor, and he prescribed sixty pills of tramadol. We picked them up from the pharmacy, but she never took any of them. She had realized just how addictive the opioids were and was adamant that she'd rather deal with the pain than go through the internal shaking of withdrawal again.

There are several categories of opioids, some natural and some synthetic. Natural opioids include morphine and codeine. Semi-synthetic opioids include oxycodone (Percocet and OxyContin), hydrocodone (Vicodin), hydromorphone, and oxymorphone. Then there are synthetic opioids like methadone, tramadol, and fentanyl.

Some opioids are illegal. Heroin is an illegally made opioid that looks like a white or brown powder or a sticky black substance. It is synthesized from morphine, but it's fifty times more potent. There are two types of fentanyl: legally made fentanyl, which doctors primarily prescribe to manage acute and chronic pain associated with advanced cancer, and illegally made fentanyl, which is often mixed with heroin and/or cocaine—with or without the user's knowledge—in order to increase the drug's effect. The illegal form of fentanyl is fifty times more potent than heroin. For more information on any of these medications, go to the Centers for Disease Control and Prevention on the Internet and click on marijuana.

The problem is called an "opioid epidemic" because prescription opioids continue to be one of the primary factors in the frightening rise in overdose deaths in general as well as those due to heroin and illegally made fentanyl. A large proportion of these deaths also show that the victim had both prescription drugs and illegal drugs present in his system.

People addicted to prescription opioids must increase the dosage over time as they naturally build up a tolerance to their effects. Maintaining that dependency on the drug can become quite expensive as well as time-consuming. Multiple prescriptions are needed (which means multiple doctors are required), or the meds must be bought on the street. Both sources require some resourcefulness on the part of the addict, and that's when people are tempted to turn to heroin, the cheaper and more readily available substitute.

That explains in part why heroin use has more than tripled since 2010, and the increase has touched every adult age group and those at all income levels. The result is that the number of deaths from heroin overdose has quadrupled as well. Almost thirteen thousand heroin overdose deaths were reported by the Centers for Disease Control in 2015. Four out of five heroin users abused prescription opioids first, and so they are not the stereotypical image of a "junkie." Heroin addiction has invaded the suburbs and the small towns across the country.

One problem that contributes to overdoses from heroin is that there is no standard dosage; it must be determined by the abuser. But the strength of heroin is "cut" by the dealer with substances like sugar or lactose—or rat poison. Any number of toxic additives can be used in order to increase the dealer's profits. The unpredictability of both its strength and its composition can make it fatal.

Recently, heroin dealers have been cutting the drug with fentanyl and synthetic opioids that are far more potent than the heroin itself. Some are even cutting it with carfentanil, a tranquiller opioid used with large animals such as horses and even elephants that is ten thousand times more potent than morphine or heroin. Some users have died with the needles still in their arms. It is more than an epidemic—it's a crisis!

Drug Dealer, MD

For the past couple of decades, opioid prescriptions for pain relief have grown at a rapid pace. Psychiatrist Anna Lembke, chief of addiction medicine at Stanford University's medical school, points out in her book, *Drug Dealer, MD*, that "prior to 1980, doctors used opioid pain relievers sparingly, and only for the short term in cases of severe injury or illness, or during surgery. Their reluctance to use opioids for an extended length of time, despite their short-term effectiveness for pain, sprang from fear of causing addiction."[1]

Few experts would agree that the treatment of pain had been inadequate. But several large pharmaceutical companies ("Big Pharma") saw this as an opportunity. According to a series of articles in the *Los Angeles Times*,[2] some pharmaceutical companies purposefully tried to get opioid medications prescribed by more

---

1   Anna Lembke, *Drug Dealer, MD* (Baltimore: John Hopkins University Press, 2016), 56–57.
2   Harriet Ryan, Lisa Girion, and Scott Glover, "OxyContin Goes Global—'We're Only Just Getting Started,'" *Los Angeles Times*, December 18, 2016.

doctors. The article points out that since sales have fallen in the United States, companies have developed a global initiative to get opioids prescribed internationally. They are using the same strategy internationally that they used to increase sales and profits in the United States.

The strategy used by Big Pharma companies involves enlisting academic physicians to teach doctors how to prescribe more opioids. They based the increase on a "fact" they and the academic doctors created between them. They teach that we have underestimated the number of people dealing with chronic pain, inflating the number of chronic pain sufferers from a realistic twenty-five million in the United States to a profit-oriented number more like one hundred million. They look through medical research for academic doctors whose limited findings favored the companies' inflated numbers and recruit them to teach the other doctors how to prescribe.

One of the other positions postulated by these academic doctors and Big Pharma is that instead of limiting opioids to short-term use, it is safe to prescribe them for long-term treatment of chronic pain. They also teach about what they called "pseudoaddiction." Lembke describes what this term means: "Based on a single case report of a patient who engaged in drug-seeking behavior due to inadequate pain control, doctors were taught that any patient prescribed opioid painkillers who demonstrates drug-seeking behavior is not addicted, but in pain."[3] In other words, they are taught to deny that it really is an addiction!

---

3   Lembke, *Drug Dealer, MD*, 61.

The consumer is not innocent in the development of the epidemic either. No one likes to live with chronic pain, so when someone offers the promise of relief, who wouldn't naturally accept it? But once a person is addicted to opioids, like any other addiction, the drug hijacks his brain. It's like when someone hasn't eaten for days: hunger takes over, and he will do almost anything to find some food. But unlike hunger, opioid addiction is extremely difficult to treat. That only compounds the problem.

Obviously, the addicted person you love may feel very alone, but the truth is, her problem is really a family problem, and treatment and recovery is a family affair as well. That means you are part of the solution that will lead to recovery and healing.

CHAPTER THREE

Addiction

A FAMILY DISEASE

At that initial group therapy meeting for my family member, I should have known what the young man meant when he pointed out that I also had a problem: I was as much a part of the problem as anyone, and *our* problem wasn't going to be resolved until I dealt with my own problem.

Part of my training as a counselor had been to understand how a family works—and how it doesn't work. A family is more than a group of individuals who happen to share the same address and the same last name. It is an interconnected system of people, each of whom affects all the others. I had to step back and personalize that truth and see that our obvious problem was part of a system of relationships and interpersonal dynamics that involved, and even centered on, me. What that meant was that if the behavioral family system could be changed, then the problem itself would change. And it was up to everyone in the family to begin working toward that.

In the late 1950s, psychotherapists made a remarkable discovery about families. Up to that point, therapists had been governed by both ethical and theoretical principles that only allowed treatment between one patient and one therapist. Therefore, professional marital therapy and family therapy did not exist. However, there was a lot of grant money available to study schizophrenic patients, and some of the studies were designed to observe the patient in the context of her family.

Some researchers moved the whole family into the hospital to observe them 24-7. Dad could go to work and the kids could go to school, but for a period of time, the family lived in the hospital. All the researchers worked with the family as a whole.

What they started to see was amazing. Much of the patient's schizophrenic behavior, when looked at individually, was clearly a disorder. But when observed within the context of the family, it could be seen as perfectly reasonable. In other words, the problem wasn't just an individual problem; it was also a family problem. And the patient's behavior, which was the focus of the study, served some purpose within the dynamics of the family. Family therapy became a standard practice after that.

When the studies with schizophrenia were finished, grant money became available to study the families of alcoholics to see if there were similar patterns of behavior. When those studies were finished, the researchers found the same results. Alcoholism, like schizophrenia in the earlier study, was found to serve some kind of purpose within the family. It also showed that addiction and alcoholism were family disorders or diseases.

That means that the behavior of the addict/alcoholic is only one element of the dysfunctional pattern in the family and is connected to each and every family member. I've worked with alcoholic families where the active alcoholic got into recovery and stopped drinking, but when the family didn't do their part, it didn't take very long for one of them to at least become a problem drinker. The unrecovered family still needed someone to have a problem with alcohol or an addiction. I've also worked with alcoholic families that found that when they actively focused as a family on the issue, the addict's recovery was inevitable and the family as a whole became healthier.

In my family, I found out that I was not only part of the problem; I played the role of what is called "the dependent." It was like I was the addict/alcoholic (even though I wasn't) because the family problem revolved around me. In an earlier treatment program's family week, a friend set our family up in what's called a "family sculpture." This is an activity where different people take on the roles played by each family member—or in our case, the members of the family actually acted out how the friend saw our family.

The friend sat me in the middle with the other family members in a circle around me. I was directed to be preoccupied with reading a book. Jan was portrayed as the codependent/enabler, busy running around intercepting anyone who tried to get my attention. One son was busy at work, so he stood with his back to me; another son was bouncing around the outskirts of the circle, saying, "I'm here, I'm here!" What we found out from the sculpture of our family was that if there was to be change in our family, it would need to start with me, and it would also have to include everyone. What an eye-opener that was for the whole family!

Linear and Interactive Thinking

So the family is the context for the problem of the addict/ alcoholic—but how do we begin to think through what this statement means? Here's some of what researchers have discovered about how families work and don't work in the face of an addiction/ alcoholism. I remember learning in a high school physics class the rubric that "for every action, there is an equal and opposite reaction." It's an example of "linear thinking," and it works if you are playing pool or if you are doing scientific research. But it doesn't work with family relationships.

What works in families is different. It is what is called "interactive thinking," or "circular thinking." It basically means that for any action, there are multiple causes at work, and the reactions are very unpredictable. In my book *Forgiving Our Parents, Forgiving Ourselves*, I give the following illustrations.

Linear thinking is like kicking a tin can: it's easy to predict the outcome. Interactive or circular thinking is like kicking a sleeping dog: there could be any of several outcomes. The dog might ignore you, he might move, he might growl at you, or he might bite you. He may even do something totally unexpected.

Now imagine that there are also two cats sleeping alongside the dog, a parrot elsewhere in the room, and two kids playing down the hall. Now you can get a feel for the complexity of responses that are possible, as each of these actors will respond to your action in his own unpredictable way. That's more like how we should think about cause and effect in a family.

Another complicating factor is that none of our relationships work logically—they are paradoxical, which is anything but logical. You can make a good argument for why the one you love should stop his addictive behavior, and it will make logical sense to everyone except the one you want to change. That's why nagging is useless, and the harder you try to "get through" to the addict, the more everything stays the same. So stop trying to be logical. Stop nagging. Instead, work on yourself and watch what happens.

Punctuation

Anyone who has been misunderstood knows how important punctuation is. Ephesians 4:28 is often used as an example: "Let him who stole, steal no longer, but rather let him labor, working with his hands what is good" (NKJV). We can change the whole meaning of that verse by simply changing the punctuation: "Let him who stole steal. No longer let him labor working with his hands." Quite a different message, all caused by a few seemingly insignificant changes.

Look at this typical exchange between a couple: Chris explains, "She nags, and so I withdraw." Donna says, "He withdraws, and so I nag." They keep changing where the sentence begins. Chris starts with "she nags," while Donna starts with "he withdraws," and where the punctuation falls depends on the direction of their linear thinking. It leads Donna to believe that change can only take place if Chris changes. And of course, it leads Chris to believe that change can only take place if Donna changes—neither of which will ever happen if they maintain their linear thinking.

But communication patterns can follow the cyclical patterns used in interactive, or circular, thinking. It can read something like this: Donna nags and Chris withdraws and Donna nags and

Chris withdraws, and so on, and so on. We could have just as easily started with Chris withdraws and Donna nags and Chris withdraws and Donna nags, and so on, and so on. Once they see these as spiraling loops that have no beginning or end, either one of them is free to change the situation by *changing himself or herself.*

Rigid Family Roles

One of the really interesting things the researchers found when looking at families of alcoholics, and, by inference, the families of addicts, is that the unhealthier a family is, the more rigid and identifiable the assumed roles are within the family. One role is that of being the core problem: the role of the *dependent.* I was given that role in the family sculpture. I was the problem because I was preoccupied with my graduate work, even though I thought I had it all in balance within the family. But everyone else in the family was subconsciously working hard to protect me from being seen as the "real problem." When we talk about *roles,* we're not talking about issues of character or even personality. We are talking about behavioral roles.

The Dependent

The *dependent* is always the addict/alcoholic (or the rageaholic, or the workaholic, or any other "holic" in the family). He or she is the real problem. So, for example, let's say I'm the addict/alcoholic. That makes me the *dependent,* meaning that in my addiction, I am dependent on the continuation of my alcohol problem. The rest of the family, in some painful way, has also become dependent on my having a problem—that's why they are called "*codependents*." The result is that the addict/alcoholic is unconsciously protected from the reality of his problem by the rest of the family, who unconsciously conspire to keep anyone, even the dependent, from having to face the reality of the real problem.

But there are some things the family can't protect the dependent from: the shame, guilt, fear, and anger he struggles with. In a way, continuing to live with his addiction temporarily numbs those feelings. This doesn't excuse his behavior, for he is also in this role because he is addicted. And the family, even though they are participating, as we will see, gains nothing positive from the dependent continuing to be addicted.

I talked with Martha, a fifty-one-year-old woman. She told me her father had just entered a treatment program for alcoholism. I said, "That's great!" After a moment of silence, she confessed, "I had no idea he drank that much. I just thought he drank a little but was sick a lot." For decades, the whole family had been kept from the reality that her dad was an alcoholic. I asked her, "How long has he been drinking?" She answered, "I guess he started before I was born. I just never knew alcohol was the problem. I guess it finally got bad enough that my mom had to admit the truth—that he was an alcoholic." Martha grew up and became an adult who never really knew the truth. That is a well-kept family secret! Mom's job as the codependent was to keep the family secret safe, even from the children.

Secrets are what keep the family dysfunction dysfunctional. Most of us have heard the saying "the elephant in the room," but it bears repeating: When the elephant was little, we put a doily on it and a lamp. We dressed it up so no one would ask, "Why do you have an elephant in your living room?" When it grew bigger and took over the living room, still no one asked, not even the members of the family. They just knew not to ask. The individual family members respected the family secret. As we were growing up, we somehow knew to only invite friends over who wouldn't ask about the elephant. Perhaps they didn't ask because they also had strange things in their living rooms. They obviously knew we wouldn't challenge their secrets, and we knew they would keep our family's secret as well.

But what we didn't realize was that the truth is, as a family, we are only as dysfunctional and as unhealthy as our secrets. Or a better way to say it is that we are as sick as our secrets. A big part of the family experience of healing and recovery is to face the family's secrets, and that includes becoming honest about the real problem—the addiction.

The Chief Enabler

As the dependent, an addict/alcoholic, I need someone to take on the role of the *chief enabler*. This role is typically taken by a spouse and is someone who *enables* the continuation of my addiction/alcoholism by protecting me from the consequences of my drinking. They are often called the "codependent" as well, for they are also in some way dependent on the continued existence of the problem. The chief enabler is also the protector of the family's secrets, sometimes even keeping the secrets from other family members, as Martha's mom had. She may complain to and about me, nag me, and do all other kinds of futile things out of frustration. She might even get angry and pour my wine down the drain. But then, because she has in some way become dependent on my problem, she will go and buy me more alcohol. And, like Martha's mother, she will always cover for me, buying my alcohol, giving me money for "food," and faithfully calling in to my work to say I'm "sick." It sounds illogical, but this is her role as the chief enabler in a dysfunctional family.

While the dependent operates primarily out of shame and guilt, chief enablers operate out of anger. They may hide their anger by expressing it passively until they reach a point of frustration where they blow up at their dependents. They usually end up feeling like they are martyrs. What they don't see is that, in reality, they are as dependent on the problem existing as the addicts/alcoholics are dependent on their addictions. The enablers in the lives of addicts/alcoholics act out of a sincere—though misguided—sense of caring, love, and loyalty. But their motivation is also based on fear. That's why they are so good at offering "explanations" for why the addicts/alcoholics act the way they do—they are afraid to face the truth about what is really going on.

Parents will also take on this role for one or more of their kids. Like all enablers, they begin by minimizing the addictive behavior, even if they don't realize it. They financially support the ongoing problem by saying their kids need to have some money for food or gas. They may even bail out their sons or daughters in court because, as they might say, they don't want their kids "caught up in the legal system." I know firsthand—we did all those things when we faced a similar problem.

Whether it's a problem with one of your kids at home, your adult child, or your spouse, as the chief enabler, you must face the fact at some point that you have been gradually taking over the responsibilities of the dependent. That's evidence that you have fully accepted your role as the chief enabler. If the dependent is your spouse, you'll find yourself gradually becoming more parental with the dependent—taking on decisions and responsibilities the dependent is avoiding.

As the addiction grows, the dependent will become more critical of the chief enabler, putting all the blame for his problems on his spouse. He'll project his guilt, shame, and self-hatred onto her. In his growing anger, he'll criticize her looks, libido, mothering skills, spending, and even choice of friends. It will become constant, and she'll start to believe the criticism. Her self-doubt will drive her to try harder just to survive as she continues to take care of the dependent. But on the positive side, the chief enabler often gets help first for the "family disease."

The Enabler-in-Training

The children or siblings usually take the other roles. The oldest daughter often assumes the role of the *enabler-in-training*. Her training sessions occur when the chief enabler (usually her parent) gets fed up with being the enabler; the trainee steps in and takes over the task.

Sarah's story is an example. Sarah described to me what her alcoholic husband did when he was abusing alcohol: "If he didn't come home until late—which was often because of his business—I knew what lay ahead for me. He would come home sloppy drunk. Thinking I was asleep, he would just fall into bed fully dressed, and then he would invariably throw up. It was like clockwork. I would then get up, undress him, clean him up, and put clean pajamas on him. I would strip the dirty sheets off the bed and put clean sheets on it. Then I would put him to bed, all nice and clean. But I wasn't finished—then I felt I had to put everything in the washing machine and turn it on before I could go back to bed myself. I didn't want to face the dirty clothes and sheets in the morning."

"Did you ever let him know your routine?" I asked.

"Yes, every time, but he always denied what happened."

"And you had destroyed all the evidence," I responded.

She thought a while and then said, "I guess I did."

What really surprised me was what she related next: "One night, he didn't make it upstairs to bed. He stopped in the downstairs bathroom, which my daughter used. He relieved himself, threw up on the floor, and then laid down and fell asleep in his vomit. My daughter found him there when she got up in the middle of the night to use the bathroom.

"She proceeded to wake him up, take off his vomit-covered clothes, clean him up, and send him upstairs to bed. Then she cleaned up the bathroom floor and took all the dirty clothes and cleaning rags and put them in the washing machine and turned it on. Just like I would have done!" She had raised her daughter as the perfect enabler-in-training.

When I talked with Sarah again several years later, she reported that her daughter had married a nice young man, but she was afraid he was also an alcoholic. And in all likelihood, he was, for enablers-in-training usually become chief enablers when they marry.

The Hero

Every dramatic story has to have its hero, and the drama of the family of an addict/alcoholic is no exception. Usually this role falls to the oldest son. When I first encountered the description of the various family roles, I had thought that the *hero* would obviously be a doctor or a lawyer or some other successful professional in the family. But I had more to learn about family roles.

When we had an inpatient hospital program some years ago, I was leading the multifamily group, and we had a young male patient who came from a very unhealthy family. I found out he was on disability, as were his father and his younger brother. It seemed like there were a lot of physical disabilities in this family. Mom was on unemployment as well. They barely got by; they had enough to live on but nothing left over to even take care of their house and property. They couldn't afford to hire a gardener, and no one was well enough to mow the lawn.

I could imagine how the neighbors judged the family. Perhaps one neighbor would say to another, "Can you believe that family? What a bunch of losers." And then the other neighbor's response would be, "Yes, but they can't be all that bad; I've heard that the oldest son has worked for the gas company for over fifteen years, and he's even been promoted several times."

I could also imagine the mom and dad talking about their failures as parents. But then one of them would say, "Yeah, it's been rough. But look at Joe and how well he's done. We can't be that bad as parents! We got at least one right!" When I met the rest of the family, Joe, the oldest son, clearly fit the role of the family hero.

In reality, the hero's job is twofold. First, because he's successful, he often helps the family when they need help. And second, he *has to* succeed in order to make the family look good, both to the outside world and to the family itself. As is typical of many oldest children, I found that Joe was very responsible in how he lived, even in the midst of a very irresponsible family system.

Growing up, the hero probably got a lot of special attention from the extended family. But he also experiences a lot of stress, for he has carried an inordinate amount of the family tension and stress within himself. He typically tries to bury those negative feelings by working harder to succeed. In some cases, the hero acts as a parent to his or her parents—not only as an adult, but even while growing up.

The Scapegoat

This child is often the second born. While growing up, he watched his older sibling do everything the right way, so the role of being the "good" one in this crazy family was already taken. As a result, his response is to act out "badness" in some way. Eventually, within the family, the role of *scapegoat* is taken by the one whose problems we focus on, for it helps us avoid dealing with those of the dependent. This role is the reverse image of the hero's role. When the tension begins to build, the scapegoat acts out and draws the family's tension to himself.

Scapegoats may begin by pushing the limits and getting away with it. Since they typically feel like outsiders within their families, budding scapegoats are often drawn to other kids who are already acting out. Eventually, acting out escalates into causing some kind of trouble for the family.

He may get into drinking or doing drugs. He may get into other kinds of trouble with the law, such as stealing, shoplifting, or vandalism. He may become sexually active at a young age and end up involved in a pregnancy. But the unconscious purpose of this role is to take the pressure off the parent who is the "real" problem. After all, what enabler has the energy to deal both with a child who is "going bad" and a spouse whose alcohol or drug problem is already more than she can handle and only getting worse? The family's focus is on trying to fix the scapegoat—at least it feels like there is some hope there.

The cost of taking on this role in the family dysfunction is obvious. The scapegoat's self-destructive behavior puts him at risk for long-term consequences. One may wonder why he would make such a sacrifice, but his behavior is ultimately the result of feeling worthless.

I remember working with two families where, as the scapegoats got older, they grew tired of the chaos they had created in their own lives. The result was that they straightened out and gave up acting out the role of the scapegoat. In both cases, their families hadn't sought treatment, the dependents were still using or drinking, and the addicted/alcoholic families still needed someone to play the role of the scapegoat. So one of the other grown children took on the role and started getting in trouble and acting out.

The Lost Child

By the time the third child is born, the family chaos and dysfunction have increased. As this child grows, she senses the tension, but no one fills her in on what is going on. The family members don't have the time or even the ability to answer her questions because of the secrecy rule. So she chooses to get lost. She becomes a loner in the family, looking after her own needs and staying out of the way.

Typically, she is seen as a good child, since she has learned to avoid making waves. But by the same token, she is also the forgotten child. As such, she begins to isolate herself more and more from the family. The family dynamic is relieved—here's a child who doesn't add to the family tension! That's because she spends a lot of time in her own private world. But the result is that she never really learns how to relate to others or to comfortably express her own feelings. She also isn't equipped to know what to do when others express their feelings, especially negative feelings. She has little experience living life, and so when the lost child grows up, she tends to keep a low profile and is constantly aware of the feeling of being lost.

The Comic

As our play has developed thus far, we've watched the dependent become more entrenched in alcoholism, or rage, or whatever his addiction might be. Denial has been the fail-safe response to any suggestion to change. The chief enabler is running around trying to fix the dependent's problem, fix the scapegoat, and/or maintain the secrets of the family. The children become more entrenched in their increasingly clear behavioral roles, but we need one more character in our play—the *comic*, the one who tries to break the tension by bringing fun to a very unhealthy family.

It's interesting that the more unhealthy the family, the more they need someone to take on the role of the comic. Someone needs to break the tension with some humor. What I call the "comic" is also called the "mascot"—it is someone who seeks to fit in through comedy. Just when the family's problems are about to cause an explosion, the comic makes a witty comment that causes the family to laugh. They shift their attention from the problem to the relief provided by the laughter.

Many well-known comedians learned their skills as a result of growing up in a highly dysfunctional alcoholic family. Have you ever noticed that the typical painted-on clown's face has not only an artificial smile for a mouth but also a tear coming from one of the eyes? Sometimes, a person's aptitude for comedy was born from the struggles of his early life—it served a purpose then, but it became a way of life in adulthood. All through his life, comedy has been a way to hide from pain.

When we had the hospital program, we often traveled to hold seminars. For one weekend seminar, we had our emcee traveling with us, and he was hilariously funny. His job was to provide comic relief to a serious seminar, and he did it well. I talked with him on one trip and asked him about his family. He related a very difficult childhood but made the point that it was also where he had learned his humor. "What else was I supposed to do?" he asked. "Somebody had to distract from the pain."

I could have suggested that some choose to respond as a hero, a scapegoat, or a lost child, but I didn't. The conversation was too painful.

What If There Aren't Five Kids?

We've described five roles the kids in a family can play, and a good question to ask is, "What if there are only one, two, or three kids in the family?" In that case, the kids "double-up" on the roles. The hero can also be the enabler-in-training, and the scapegoat, the lost child, or even the hero can take on the role of the comic.

In our family, we have three children. In the family sculpture I described, we had a hero, a scapegoat, and a lost child. We didn't have a comic or an enabler-in-training, but sometimes, one of the kids would try to help or be funny. So, over the passage of time, our family had expressed all these behaviors.

The more unhealthy the family, the more clear and concrete the behavioral roles will be (at least to an outside observer). The more healthy the family, the more fluid and diffuse the behavioral roles will be. The purpose of describing these roles is to help you see that addiction/alcoholism is really a family disease, and everybody in the family needs help.

It's also important to note that while we sometimes ascribed a role to a particular gender, men or woman may take on any of them or their characteristics. While the hero and the scapegoat tend to be male, they could just as easily be female. The same is true for the dependent, the chief enabler, the enabler-in-training, the comic, and the lost child. Family roles have no gender bias.

The Role of Denial

You've probably heard this scenario before: someone tells an alcoholic that he is an alcoholic, the accused person strongly denies it, and the accuser says, "See? That proves you're an alcoholic. You're in denial." Of course, this is not a valid test. Sometimes what is called "denial" is really the truth. However, it is true that every addict or alcoholic is in denial about the extent of his problem.

I still remember when I first realized that the purpose of denial is not to fool others into thinking there is no problem; it's for alcoholics/addicts to fool themselves into believing the myth that *they* don't have a problem. They are not pretending—it is their strange "truth." They may know subconsciously that there is a problem, but on the conscious level, they actually believe there is no problem.

Of course, within the family, denial takes several forms. The one that I see most often is the tendency to focus on a problem other than the addiction or alcoholism. We may say that our spouse is under a lot of pressure at work and can only handle it by drinking, or a young adult who is addicted to Adderall is suffering from ADHD or depression. Or perhaps we imagine that someone only drinks because his anxiety level is so high. We'd much rather focus on and deal with some other issue rather than face the reality of an addiction.

The principle to keep in mind when getting help for the addict or alcoholic is that the addiction must be dealt with first, not the ADHD, the depression, the anxiety, or whatever else we blame for the drinking or drug use. Picture it this way: The addiction is something that takes over a person the way an alien takes over a person in the movies. So whenever you talk with that person, you are not really talking with her, you are talking with her resident alien—her addiction. If you focus on the ADHD, the anxiety, or the depression, the alien resident—the addiction—can relax; it is not the focus of the conversation. The addiction is off the hook. That's why you can't work on any other problem effectively until the addiction or alcoholism is dealt with!

So now that we know that the addiction is the primary issue and that each family member is involved in some way, let's look at what steps we can take to bring about restoration and recovery.

CHAPTER FOUR

Here's What *You* Do

Our goal is to stop being a part of the problem and to start becoming part of the resolution of the problem. And, as everyone in recovery knows, since becoming clean and sober is a spiritual journey, we have to recognize that the process that leads to sobriety and recovery is going to involve us in a spiritual battle.

Every addiction is all-encompassing. It is a physical problem—we are physically addicted in some way. It is a mental problem—what AA, NA (Narcotics Anonymous), and Al-Anon call "stinking thinking." It is an emotional problem—we are dependent on our drug of choice. And it is a spiritual problem—we have made our addiction our god. So we must be prepared spiritually as well. This is done through faithfully praying for the one we love who is addicted.

Prepare Yourselves for a Spiritual Battle

When we realized what we were up against in our family, my wife and I prayed together every night and every morning. We often withdrew our dependence on God and tried to fix things ourselves only to be reminded of our powerlessness—perhaps the hardest lesson we had to learn. Sometimes, we didn't even know how to pray beyond the words "God, please help us!" But we prayed and eventually learned that since we were in a spiritual battle, we had to continually acknowledge our dependence on God and give the one we love over to God and His care. That was the first step.

There were months when we didn't know where the addict in our family was. We didn't even know if he was dead or alive. All we could do was turn him over to God's care through daily prayer. We had other people praying and other churches praying—even one in Australia that prayed regularly for him. We fought the spiritual battle through continual prayer; that's where the recovery of the one you love always begins.

Get Educated

Step two is to get educated. As I said earlier, I started learning about addiction as a young pastor working with the family of an alcoholic. At that point, my education involved confronting some of my ignorance of alcoholism. When I went to graduate school in preparation to become a psychologist, there weren't any courses offered on addiction—the subject was totally absent. When addiction hit our family, we tried to get help, but we couldn't find anyone who really knew how to help. At that time, counselors and psychiatrists had little or no training in the treatment of addiction. Even one of the leading addiction specialists didn't know what to do with our family. At the end of the session, he told us, "I don't know how to help you. You don't fit the mold." This was in the 1970s.

While it felt sort of good that we didn't fit the mold, we still needed help. While it is important to note here that reading books, articles, Internet postings, and other material can be helpful, it is not nearly as powerful as hearing stories from actual people who have worked through a program and found sobriety. For us as a family, it was several years later that we started our real education, when we were all put in a treatment program that required us to attend a specific AA speaker meeting every Monday night for six months. Remember, in these types of meetings, the only one who shares is the speaker. Those in attendance don't speak; they listen and learn. We came in, sat down, and listened to someone's story. When the story was finished, we got up and went home. That's the way it works. We did this in 1986, and some of the stories were so powerful, I still remember them to this day.

One story was told by a priest who described a time when he was in Mexico and having brunch at a restaurant. He was eating on the outdoor patio, in the center of which was a flowing fountain of margaritas—all you could drink. Once you paid for a glass, you could fill it as often as you wanted. He told us how he reached a point where he just had to get out of there. He left with his brunch only half-eaten. When he finished the story, he added what, to me, was the most memorable part: "I imagine that as they lay me down in my coffin, my addiction will be there beside me. And just before they close the lid, my addiction will sit up and say to me, 'Come on, Joe, let's have one more for the road!'" That was the power of his alcohol addiction.

The doctor at the treatment center led the meetings. He told us about the problems with alcoholism in the medical community, and I remember a cardiologist who spoke. He was on the faculty of a well-known medical school, and his story was about how he developed a more advanced procedure for implanting a pacemaker in a patient. He said, "I was called in for an emergency to implant a pacemaker, and I had been drinking way too much to do such a procedure. But no one knew I had a problem, and I wasn't about to make my problem known." So he did a partial implant and said to himself that he would come back in the morning to finish the task. The next morning, he was amazed to find that what he called a "partial implant" was an improvement on the current procedure, and his "too drunk to do it right" version became the standard for a time. He wasn't proud of this accomplishment, for he was quick to say that he now practices sobriety.

When a family comes to me because they are dealing with the addiction of someone they love, I tell them that if they want my help, they need to attend the Saturday evening speaker meeting at the local hospital. They are to take as many of their family members with them as possible, then go out for coffee after the meeting and talk together about what they heard. Not every speaker's story will be relevant to their family, but the purpose is to get educated about addictions and alcoholism.

Tom came to see me because his wife was fed up with his "cocktail hour." Every evening at five, he mixed, poured, and drank several cocktails, just as his parents had every evening while he was growing up. And like his parents, only part of him was really present during the rest of the evening. He wasn't drunk, just not fully there. Tom's wife was convinced he was an alcoholic, but he wanted my opinion. I told him I thought his drinking was obviously causing problems, but then I added, "I can't diagnose whether you are an alcoholic or not, but here's what I want you to do while seeing me. I want you to attend a weekly speaker meeting, and the best one I know about is Saturday evenings at the local hospital."

Tom went to a speaker meeting, but not the one at the hospital. He had called and gotten a list of AA meetings, and on that list, speaker meetings were included. He decided on a meeting near his home and went every week as I had suggested. I think it was after the fifth week that he came in for his counseling appointment with me and announced, "I'm an alcoholic." The meetings had bypassed his denial system, and he recognized himself in the speakers' stories.

I've had parents take their teenagers to the meeting—even those who weren't heading down the path of addiction. It becomes an excellent way to talk with your teens about the dangers and maybe even their propensity for addiction based on your family's history. Listening together and talking about what you heard at the meeting helps get you all on the same page.

How do you find a good speaker meeting? Begin by contacting a local hospital that has an addiction treatment program. Your hospital may sponsor a quality program because it is also a marketing tool for their treatment course. If that doesn't work, get on the Internet and search for "AA meetings." You will get a list of states—click on your state and then find your closest AA office's phone number. Call and ask them to send you a list of local meetings. It will probably arrive in a plain envelope. Then pick your meeting site and attend at least six meetings—more if you like. And don't forget, the key is to talk together about what you heard.

So step one is to pray for the addict/alcoholic and for the family of the addict/alcoholic. The second step is to get educated by finding a speaker meeting and attending it together with as many family members as possible. Be sure to talk together about what you heard.

Get into an Addiction Support Group

Step three is to get into a support group that understands addictions and alcoholism. There are a variety of Al-Anon and Christian recovery support groups. When I work with a family where a teen or a grown child is struggling with a drug or alcohol addiction, I tell them about a special Al-Anon group that more than one hundred parents typically attend early every Saturday morning. These parents have either a grown son or daughter who is still actively addicted or is in recovery. After they have attended, I get mixed reviews of their impressions.

Amy, whose daughter is addicted to Adderall, told me after attending her first meeting, "I can't go back there. Those people don't even care about their children. They were laughing and having a good time together." I had to explain to her that they still cared deeply, but because of the support they felt from the others in the group, they had learned they couldn't do anything directly to help their addicted offspring and were in the process of taking their own lives back. Since they had learned how to give up responsibility for their kids' behavior, they were discovering they still had their own lives. I'm not sure she believed me, as she just shook her head and said, "That's nice."

I had already explained to her that she needed to go four or five times at least to understand the difference between her life and their lives. She didn't go for a week or two, but then she started to go regularly and talked with some of the other parents, and in hearing their stories, she started to understand what it meant to be an enabler.

Marty, whom you met in the first chapter, started going to Al-Anon while I helped her understand her enabling behaviors. Her group was very supportive of her, and as she worked with me and listened to the stories of those married to active alcoholics, she gradually started to change her behavior patterns. Later, when Robert got into treatment, she sincerely felt that her changes were part of the reason. She also began to understand that even though they weren't married yet, she was still a part of the "family disease" of alcoholism. Both she and Amy had to understand that they were part of the problem and needed to help themselves in order to become part of the resolution.

I am aware of several good Al-Anon meetings, which I suggest to people, but I also tell them they need to go to several different meetings in order to find one that fits. We usually can sense when we feel like we fit in with a group of people. Just like finding a speaker meeting, you can go to the Internet and look up "Al-Anon meetings," then click on your state, find the phone number for your local chapter, and ask them to send you a list of local meetings. They also list the Alateen groups, which are geared toward adolescents.

Some people aren't sure about going to a "secular" AA or Al-Anon meeting. I know a number of Christians who worried about this but went anyway—and they found the support they needed. But in recent years, specifically Christian support groups have grown and are available pretty much everywhere. To find a Christian support group near you, you can call 800-NEW-LIFE (800-639-5433) and ask for the nearest Life Recovery Group. In one of the families I have worked with, the parents attend "secular" Al-Anon meetings while their recovering alcoholic daughter attends only Christian meetings, and they find no conflicts between what they are learning and what she is learning. And it's working—a family in recovery!

Some wonder why being in a Bible study group isn't enough. But the focus of most Bible studies is to learn more about the Bible, and while sometimes that includes working on what the Bible means in our lives, it usually does not focus on the principles we need to learn regarding sobriety and recovery. If you are already in a good Bible study, stay involved there, but you need to add the speaker meetings and Al-Anon groups as well.

I also found over the years that you don't need to limit yourself to a Christian recovery group. Al-Anon exists for a singular purpose. Those who attend are there to "help themselves and others overcome the frustration and helplessness caused by living or having lived with an alcoholic,"[4] and one could add, "or addict." But as with any self-help type of group, the quality of the groups will vary. That's why I say that if a meeting seems useless to you and the people are only sitting around complaining, don't go back. Find a group whose focus is on being supportive to those in attendance.

---

4   *Living with an Alcoholic with the Help of Al-Anon* (New York: Al-Anon Family Group Headquarters, 1980), Introduction.

Your goal is to benefit from the meeting, feel like you are learning different ways to behave, and discover what you need to be supported.

"Should I tell the addict/alcoholic that I am going to start attending Al-Anon?" The answer to that question is a resounding "Yes!" But be careful how you say it. Here's how I suggest you say it: "I'm going to go to an Al-Anon meeting tonight (or today), and I'm going because I need to get help for myself." You will probably be met with some resistance, but all you need do is repeat the statement "I need to get some help for myself."

Why would the addict/alcoholic resist your decision to go to Al-Anon? Because deep down inside, they know that if you get help for yourself, their days of active addiction/alcoholism are numbered. You need the support of a group regardless of the resistance you encounter. Keep the focus on "I need help for me." It's important that you do not keep your attendance at Al-Anon, or whatever support group you are attending, a secret from the addict/alcoholic you love.

What's Next?

Hopefully, in your journey of personal recovery, you have learned that your behaviors have been designed to protect the addict/alcoholic from the consequences of their addictive behaviors. The story of Anne and Gary illustrates this.

Anne and Gary told me they had lost count of how many times they had bailed their addicted son out of jail and paid the lawyers out of their own pocket. They described one time when they were sitting in an attorney's office, and the attorney asked their son how he was going to pay. When the son said he didn't know how, the attorney asked him if he had a car. When he said he had an old VW, the attorney said, "I'll take that in payment."

Both Anne and Gary said they have never forgotten the look they got from the attorney, who also happened to be a friend, when Gary stepped in and said, "No, that won't be necessary. We will pay your fee." It was then that they realized they desperately needed more education. Gary said, "I wasn't thinking 'consequences for him,' I was thinking 'consequences for me.' I was thinking how inconvenient it would be to have to drive him around." Changes in their son didn't come until both Anne and Gary made some changes in themselves. They got educated!

Ted told the story of how he and his wife, after several years of education and support in practicing tough love, had to call the police to report that some of his wife's jewelry was missing. The police officer asked, "Could one of your kids have done this?" and put his pen in his pocket and closed his report folder. But Ted told me, "When we said 'Yes, and if it's true, we are committed to pressing charges,' the officer got out his pen, opened his folder, and finished taking the report." One of Ted's kids was guilty—he had pawned the jewelry—and Ted said his son spent the next nine months in jail as he and his wife followed through and pressed charges.

Ted said it was one of the hardest things he ever had to do, but they now understood how their son's addiction was a family issue. Neither he nor his wife could have done it without the support of their Al-Anon group or the principles of codependency they had begun to understand. He added, "We became more believable to our son after that, and it was part of the beginning of change in our family."

Whatever our motivation—be it sympathy, fear, or a need to feel, in some way, in control—codependency is a universal response to the problems created by the addiction or the alcoholism. What we need to understand is that our natural response is called "enabling behavior," and it only perpetuates the problem it is meant to solve.

Think back to the example of Marty in the first chapter. Everything she did for Robert was motivated by her love and concern for him. What could be wrong with fixing him meals? What could be wrong with buying his wine for him and keeping him from needing to drive to the store? Her behaviors made sense because she was trying to "act natural." But all those behaviors only made it possible for Robert to stay lost in his alcoholism.

Learning about how our enabling behaviors only perpetuate the problem is essential. We need to learn how to think and act differently. Like Sarah, our first thoughts are "But I care. I love him!" But genuine love seeks to bring health and recovery to our addict/ alcoholic, and we must learn that our natural way of showing love and care doesn't work with an addict/alcoholic. That's part of why it's called "tough love."

Tough Love

I've encountered a lot of people who misunderstand what *tough love* is and how to express it. Our enabling behavior typically ignores the word *tough* because we are motivated by a love that, unfortunately, only perpetuates the problem. Or our enabling behavior ignores the word *love* and just focuses our frustration on being tough, and so we have no credibility because we just end up acting angry and mean-spirited. To bring both words—*tough* and *love*—into play, let's go back to the beginning of this chapter and remind ourselves that tough love is built on a lot of prayer—especially prayer for understanding and protection.

Our problem with finding a balance with tough love is that the two words seem contradictory. How can I be tough while I am being loving? To do this, you need to express your toughness in loving ways and your loving behaviors must have a toughness to them. That's why Anne and Gary said to their son, "If anything disappears from the house, we will call the police and press charges." When he faced a jail term, they said, "We're sorry, and we still love you, but we also warned you." Tough love means we set the boundaries, and when they are violated, we still affirm our love as we enforce the boundary.

If we do it right, we put the burden of the interpretation of our tough-love message on the listener. We are tough in that we will do what we said we would do, *and* at the same time, we genuinely reaffirm our love. Now the addict/alcoholic is faced with a quandary: Does she believe the tough message about the boundary, or does she believe the love message? Until she starts to pay attention to what you're saying, she will usually believe only one side of the dual message—and typically, it's the loving side. She is surprised that you meant the boundary side of the message as well. Whichever part of the message the addict/alcoholic responds to, reaffirm the other side: If she hears only the love message, repeat the tough message. If she hears only the tough message, repeat the love message.

To be an example of tough love, the message must also be both kind and firm at the same time. That was a hard truth for my family to grasp. Typically, when I was tough, my wife tried to balance it with love. And those times when she got fed up and was tough, I took the kind role and tried to balance it all. All that did was give our loved one a choice of who to listen to and let him play each of us against the other. Everyone needs to be on the same page when practicing tough love.

Tough love also means not making threats you can't carry out. There's no room for empty threats in tough love. You also have to stop nagging the addict/alcoholic. Nagging only leads to arguments and increased tension. And probably hardest of all, to practice tough love, you must not be afraid of losing the addict/alcoholic. You may lose him for a while, but he will almost always come back. Of course, there is also a real risk of losing him for good, but that's when you must have enough support around you to make you face the reality that you are powerless anyway and must stay the course.

When All Else Fails

So you've done all of the above. You've been to speaker meetings and you're in Al-Anon as well as in a Life Recovery Group. You've even become adept at tough love and stopped at least most of your enabling behaviors. But the problems remain the same. "What now?" you desperately ask. "Do we just let the addict/alcoholic continue on her path of self-destruction? Do we just give up until the addict/alcoholic hits rock bottom or dies?"

Intervention

Fortunately, there is another step we can take. An *intervention* is designed to help the addict/alcoholic hit a "false bottom" before he hits the real bottom. It is a relatively simple event, but to be effective, it requires careful planning and professional help from someone who understands the dynamics of an intervention, as well as the dynamics of any addiction. Sometimes people try to do an intervention without getting professional help, and it often only makes things worse. When that happens, the family members pay the price—their source of hope suddenly crashes and burns. So it pays to use a professional.

In an intervention, family, friends, coworkers, and any other important people in the addict/alcoholic's life lovingly confront the addict/alcoholic for the purpose of getting her to agree to begin treatment. Each person brings evidence of how the addict/alcoholic's behavior has hurt him in hopes that the accumulation of evidence from everyone present will break through the addict/alcoholic's denial and she will agree to go into treatment immediately.

While it takes only one wavering person to undercut and destroy the intervention, it also takes only one person to get an intervention started. Here are some guidelines:

1. Once you are ready to start preparing for an intervention, you need to recruit a trained interventionist or a knowledgeable counselor. This isn't as hard as it sounds. When you research the treatment center you want to use, ask if

they can provide or refer you to a trained interventionist. This person will train the participants and guide everyone during the actual confrontation with the addict/alcoholic and will know how to remain objective, especially if the situation becomes volatile.

2. Choose who you will have on the intervention team. Each team member needs to be close to the addict/alcoholic in some way. Family members, of course, are on the team. So are close friends who understand the problem. If appropriate, a boss, along with any close coworkers, and a minister should be included. Your children should also be included regardless of their ages. It is also helpful to have someone on the team who is both a recovering addict or alcoholic and a friend.

   An important question is who *not* to include. Eliminate anyone whose mental state is not steady enough to handle the emotional impact of the intervention. You don't want to include anyone who has a tendency to preach, moralize, or berate. And you want to exclude anyone who directs a lot of anger toward the addict/alcoholic or has a deep-seated grudge against him or her. Overall, the optimal size of an intervention team would be around six to eight people, including the interventionist. But follow the guidance on numbers suggested by your professional.

3. Have the professional fill in the gaps in everyone's understanding of the addiction as a disease. Make sure that

everyone understands the family roles (outlined in
Chapter 3) and how addiction has impacted the family.

4. Plan and have a practice session, but before having your
    practice session, have everyone make a list of how the
    addict/alcoholic's behavior has impacted them. This can
    include any young children, but you will need to help
    them make their lists. The professional will help you
    phrase your list in the best possible way. There must be
    no hint of hostility or finger-pointing in what you say
    during the intervention. After everyone's lists have been
    checked, be sure you practice presenting your statements.
    Practicing helps calm the nerves and increases our confi-
    dence that the intervention will be effective. When you
    feel you are ready, set and confirm the time for the actual
    intervention.

It is important that you pray together for God to help each
of you do your best and that the intervention will be effective.
Surround the whole process with prayer, spending time during
all of your preparations in prayer. If one of my family members
was the focus of the intervention, I would also want to recruit a
team of people who would agree to be praying during the actual
time of the intervention. You may also want to open and close the
intervention with prayer.

Along the way, you will have to decide what the desired outcome
is. It might be that the addict/alcoholic will agree to go inpatient
to a thirty-day treatment program or do an outpatient program or

ninety AA or NA meetings in ninety days. These would all be considered successes. Another possible success would be for the addict/alcoholic to promise to quit on his own. Even though he has tried and failed at this in the past, this time, get a verbal and written contract in the meeting that says that if he uses or drinks again, he will immediately go into treatment. If done in a loving way, it can set the addict/alcoholic up to actually go into treatment when he realizes he really can't stop on his own.

What If the Intervention Fails?

What are the consequences if the addict/alcoholic refuses to go into treatment? This should be covered and agreed on in advance under the direction of your professional. Think through how you will handle your loved one's refusal to get help. One option is to repeat the intervention. Sometimes what doesn't work the first time works the second time. Leave some time between the two interventions so the addict/alcoholic can think about what was said the first time. There will be an increase in the addict/alcoholic's anxiety after the first intervention. Just give it some time to build.

Above all, don't devalue what seems at this point to be an unsuccessful intervention. There can be all kinds of residual benefits. For the family, it usually is a time of healing. It is also a time of education. Many times, another family member comes to realize she also has a problem. So if you're looking at what seems like a failed intervention, know that interventions are seldom wasted.

This also gives you an opportunity to see how powerful denial as a defense really is. How can a person sit through a litany of painful incidents that people he loves have experienced at his hands and still deny he has a problem? If that happens, it's important to remember that his denial is not him talking, it's the addiction talking. Get the addiction out of the picture, and you will get your loved one back.

CHAPTER FIVE

The Healing Journey

If you and your addicted/alcoholic loved one were living a hundred years ago, your predicament would be considered hopeless apart from a miracle. Alcoholics were typically kept undercover in the privacy of the home or simply locked in a jail cell until they sobered up. When they did, they were released—only to repeat the process days later. Miracle deliverances seldom happened. There were no treatment programs, nor were there 12 Steps—no one had even thought of those things at that point. Even though Dr. Trotter called it a disease, there was no known way to cure the disease.

Imagine you are alive in 1937, and the one you love is addicted to alcohol. You hear of what is going on in Akron, Ohio. Hopeless alcoholics are being transformed. They are experiencing the impossible—they are becoming and staying sober! So you check it out and find there is a doctor—a beloved doctor—who had a major problem with alcohol. He's a man called Dr. Bob Smith (better known today simply as Dr. Bob, one of the cofounders of 12 Steps).

Dr. Bob was a believer who was deeply involved in a Bible study that met as part of the Oxford Group. But that didn't stop him from drinking. The members of the group were concerned about how he would drink so much and then perform surgery. One time, during a surgery that his friends had tried to convince him not to do (based in part on their concerns), he determined to stop drinking. At about the same time, he met the cofounder of AA, another seemingly hopeless drunk called Bill W. They helped each other in sobriety as they attempted to live out the Oxford Group's Four Absolutes: *absolute honesty, absolute purity, absolute unselfishness,* and *absolute love.* Their resolve was strengthened as they helped others find the sobriety they themselves were experiencing. Together, they started to have some success in helping others become sober.

Word spread, and Bill W.'s group started to meet in New York City while Dr. Bob's group continued to grow in Akron. Dr. Bob had a special room at the hospital where he supervised the detox of anyone interested in sobriety. If you wanted to stay sober, you became a potential newcomer to Dr. Bob's group. After detoxing, Dr. Bob would take you upstairs to what the members called the "surrender room." You would be asked two questions: "Do you believe in God?" and "Have you given your life to Jesus Christ as Lord and Savior?" If you couldn't answer both questions, you got down on your knees, literally, and invited Jesus Christ to take control of your life. If you wouldn't do that, Dr. Bob believed you weren't ready for recovery. Making the basis of sobriety spiritual led to a 93 percent success rate in sobriety in those early years.

Those in recovery at the time before the 12 Steps followed six principles, which became the foundation for the 12 Steps. The six principles were these:

—We admitted we were licked.

—We got honest with another person.

—We talked it over with another person.

—We made amends to those we had harmed.

—We tried to carry the message to others with no thought of reward.

—We prayed to whatever god we thought there was.

If you're familiar with the 12 Steps, you can see the way they carry over from these six principles. The 12 Steps eventually emerged after hours of discussions between Dr. Bob, Bill W., and a minister named Reverend Sam Shoemaker. They said they focused on the Bible—three parts of the Bible in particular: the Sermon on the Mount (Matt. 5–7), the book of James, and First Corinthians 13. So in the early days, Christ was the center of recovery.[5]

When Steve Arterburn and I coedited the *Life Recovery Bible* back in 1991, it was an attempt to return the 12 Steps to their biblical roots. We wanted to bring recovery back to the Bible, where it all began. In all likelihood, the addict/alcoholic you love will be working the 12 Steps in their healing once they get into treatment. But the 12 Steps aren't just for the addict/alcoholic. The family members should work on the steps as well so that they can recover from the family disease of addiction.

In addition, we firmly believe the 12 Steps are for anyone and everyone. In fact, when someone cannot afford counseling, we

---

5   See Alcoholics Anonymous, *Dr. Bob and the Good Oldtimers: A Biography, with Recollections of Early A. A. in the Midwest* (New York: Alcoholics Anonymous World Services, 1980).

suggest they go to an Al-Anon meeting and work through the 12 Steps. *Recovery* is really just another word for the biblical principles of being a disciple of Jesus. They are for you as well! Let's look at what the 12 Steps do to facilitate healing.

Steps 1–3: The First Commitment

The 12 Steps call on a person to make three commitments. First, we make a commitment to God. Second, we make a commitment to know ourselves. And third, we make a commitment to others. We'll begin by looking at the first commitment.

Step 1 is a statement of the reality of being addicted or of living with someone who is an addict/alcoholic: *We admitted that we were powerless over alcohol (or our dependencies)—that our lives had become unmanageable.* Here, we begin with the recognition that our lives are out of control and all of our efforts to control things have been ineffective. Nothing has changed, and it is only getting worse. We are overwhelmed by our feeling of powerlessness.

The recognition of our powerlessness is a foundational truth of recovery. I personally struggled for a long time with this principle. I could see myself as "powerless, but …" There had to be something I could do. I kept finding out that there is no powerlessness when it's followed by a *but*. The *but* is only my attempt to say that I do have some power, and I am therefore no longer powerless.

Think of this first step in terms of our salvation. As a believing Christian, I have to understand that I am a sinner and that there is nothing I can do by myself that will solve my problem with sin. It doesn't mean I don't try. I try to be "good enough"—I try to be a good, moral person, but I'm still a sinner. As a foundational truth, I need to accept my powerlessness over my problem with sin. The basis of my salvation is that there is *nothing* I can do by myself to solve it. I need help! And in the same way, every one of us is powerless to solve our problem with addiction/alcoholism by ourselves. We need help.

Since we are powerless, we need to find a power source, and that leads us to Step 2: *We came to believe that a Power greater than ourselves could restore us to sanity.* I remember a young man who was trying to avoid God as he tried to identify his "higher power." He was faithfully going to meetings and was beginning to work the steps. I asked him to tell me about his higher power. He told me about this gigantic tree that was outside of where one of his AA meetings was being held. He said that tree was going to be his higher power. I asked him how he was going to be empowered by that inanimate tree. It could be an inspiration, but where was the power? When he couldn't answer me, I think we went on to talk about something else.

The next week, I asked him how that tree had helped him during the week. He laughingly said he had gotten the point the previous week. He went on to tell me that his higher power now was going to be some part of himself that had power. Again, I challenged him by reminding him that a genuine higher power had to be more powerful than anything in him. Since he had also told me earlier he wasn't ready for any "God stuff," I suggested he make his AA group his initial higher power. There can be power that is greater than ourselves in a group of caring people if we let them have that power. He agreed, but inside, I prayed he would find God as his higher power.

Why settle for the group as your higher power when you have access to the ultimate power source in the whole universe, the one who also empowered the founders of AA, Jesus Christ? When you read the gospels with fresh eyes, you don't see a Jesus who is what we would consider to be "gentle, meek, and mild." There is no meekness to what happened in the Garden of Gethsemane as Judas brought the temple guards and the Roman soldiers to arrest Jesus. Jesus asks them who they are looking for, and they say, "Jesus the Nazarene." When He simply answers, "I Am he," the eyewitness John relates that "they all drew back and fell to the ground!" (see John 18:1–11). Remember, those who fell to the ground were Roman soldiers, who feared nothing. But Jesus simply says three words, and they back up and fall down. That's a powerful Jesus! Who better than Jesus to be our higher power?

Step 3 brings us to an action step: *We made a decision to turn our will and our lives over to the care of God.* Whatever your understanding of God, that is where you begin. You may be angry with God, distant from God, even have a "maybe God exists, but I don't know that He cares" attitude—but that's where you start. That's why the founders added the words "as you understand Him." We all begin with some incomplete understanding of who God is, and the point is to grow in our experience of God from that point.

But notice also that this step doesn't just ask that you turn over your life. It demands you turn over your will as well. I remember, while growing up, hearing pastors tell us to turn our lives over to

God. I tried that many times, all to no avail. I think now that the idea of turning my life over to God was too abstract. I didn't know what it meant to turn my life over beyond becoming a missionary. But if they had urged me to turn my *will* over to God, that would have been specific. There is no way of misunderstanding what it means to turn my will, my decisions, and my choices over to God: it means a life of obedience.

Only God can restore us to sanity. And the only thing required is that we are willing to obey Him and keep our eyes on Him. The writer of the book of James—one of the sources for the 12 Steps—tells us to "get rid of all the filth and evil in your lives, and humbly accept the word God has planted in your hearts, for it has the power to save your souls. But don't just listen to God's word. You must do what it says. Otherwise, you are only fooling yourselves" (Jas. 1:21–22).

Steps 4–7: The Second Commitment

Once we respond to the first commitment and are beginning to understand the reality of turning our will and our lives over to the care of God, we come to the second commitment: to know ourselves. This is an essential commitment for the addict/alcoholic we love, but it is also an essential step for the extended family to experience. It is a major part of our process of stepping out of the rigid roles we have taken in our families. Remember, addictions are a family disease.

The prophet Jeremiah tells us to "test and examine our ways" (Lam. 3:40). The apostle Paul urges us to "be honest in your evaluation of yourselves" (Rom. 12:3). Step 4 tells us, *We made a searching and fearless moral inventory of ourselves.* To be searching and fearless, we are to look at the moral issues of our lives. It's what Jesus wants from us when He says, "Why worry about a speck in your friend's eye when you have a log in your own?" Try to picture what that would literally look like. Then Jesus continues, "First get rid of the log in your own eye; then you will see well enough to deal with the speck in your friend's eye" (Matt. 7:3, 5).

This step has its origins in the Four Absolutes of the Oxford Group. Our personal inventory is meant to help us honestly know ourselves. It should begin with where we have fallen short on honesty, purity, unselfishness, and love. Where have we been dishonest and with whom? Where have we been lax in terms of our morals and our purity? When have we been selfish or unloving? We don't have to think of every instance when we have failed—that would take forever. The point is to identify patterns of behavior that we want to own and ones we want to change.

For example, instead of acting out your typical enabling behaviors, make an inventory of representative behaviors that give you a picture of why you have traditionally done these things. You get a picture of what you need to change in yourself in order to be caring but not enabling.

Another way you can get started on an inventory is to begin with a list of your resentments. After you make your list, go back over it and identify your part in the situation. This becomes the content of your inventory.

For example, as a seminar professor, I had a student who gave me a bad review. He had been a problem in the class, and I resented his negative evaluation of me. But as I reflected on the situation, I remembered that his main frustration with me had been that I had not handed out an extensive syllabus for the class. I remembered how I had made light of his concern, both to him and in my own mind. There it was! Making light of someone else's concern—I began to see this as a pattern in my behavior. I didn't do that in my counseling office, but I did it at other times. So it went on my inventory.

Once we have our inventory, we are ready for Step 5. It is a humbling experience: *We admitted to God, to ourselves, and to another person the exact nature of our wrongs*. We need to be honest with God, even though we know He knows everything. He simply wants us to tell Him. We need to be honest with ourselves, for if we aren't honest with ourselves, nothing will change. And then comes the action: sharing it all with someone we trust.

Part of the healthiness of the early church was that people acted on what James had written: "Confess your sins to each other and pray for each other so that you may be healed" (Jas. 5:16). That was their practice. Over time, as the church developed more structure, listening to confessions gradually became the domain of a priest, and the habit of confessing sins to each other disappeared. Then the sixteenth-century thinkers of the Reformation declared that we don't need a priest to confess to, for we can bypass the priest—and anyone else—and go directly to God with our confession; no human listener is needed. But the Oxford Group was different, and the 12 Steps are different: we are also to confess to another person. According to James, that's where healing takes place.

So far, we have three actions to perform: (1) turn our will and our lives over to the care of God, (2) make a fearless moral inventory of ourselves, and (3) admit to another person our wrongs. Step 6 gives us time to reflect and become willing to take the fourth action. It says, *We were entirely ready to have God remove all those defects of character.* We take no action in this step except to prepare for God to act. Once again, James helps us understand. He writes, "Humble yourselves before the Lord, and he will lift you up in honor" (Jas. 4:10).

When we are willing to let go of our wrongs, we prayerfully move to Step 7, which states, *We humbly asked God to remove our shortcomings*—but only when we are willing and ready. If we waver on the willingness and readiness, we might ask God to remove a certain shortcoming but then take it back from Him. These commitments are meant to become a daily way for us to live our lives.

Steps 8–9: The Third Commitment

We already started some of our work on Step 8 when we made our personal inventory. Looking back over that inventory, we are prepared for the third commitment, which is to make things right in our relationships with others. Step 8 says, *We made a list of all the persons we had harmed and became willing to make amends to them all*. This step is based on the passage in Matthew called the Sermon on the Mount. The Sermon on the Mount is the record of Jesus's teaching while He was in Galilee.

As part of the background to what Jesus is teaching, it is important to know that if someone was going to leave Galilee to go to Jerusalem, it would take him three days to make the journey. Keep that in mind as Jesus tells His listeners, and us, about how important it is for us to make things right with others. He says, "If you are offering your gift at the altar [in Jerusalem] and there remember that your brother or sister [back in Galilee] has something against you, leave your gift there in front of the altar. First go and be reconciled to them; then come and offer your gift" (Matt. 5:23, 24 NIV).

Here's how important Jesus's teaching is. In this example, imagine that I am to go to Jerusalem to offer a sacrifice as an act of worship. It takes me three days to get to Jerusalem. But just as I'm about ready to offer my sacrifice, I suddenly remember I have something important to take care of back home. I've offended someone, and I haven't made it right with them. There's no way I can offer the sacrifice and then make things right after I get home. That would invalidate my offering. No, this is so important that I must leave my offering in Jerusalem and take the three-day journey back home. Once I take whatever time is necessary to make things right with my brother or sister, then I make the three-day journey back to Jerusalem. Only then am I free to offer my sacrifice.

This third commitment was so important that Jesus's listeners were taught and believed that their sacrifices wouldn't truly be accepted unless they had made things right with others as much as possible.

That leads us to Step 9: *We made direct amends to such people wherever possible, except when to do so would injure them or others.* It is important to remember that at Step 3, we surrendered our lives and our will to the care of God, so all that remains is the question of whether it will do harm if we seek to make amends.

We must come to Step 9 with an attitude of prayer and humility. We also need to talk with trusted people in order to understand how and why seeking to make amends with someone could cause additional hurt and harm; we don't want to use that as an excuse to avoid it.

I've talked with a lot of people over the years who have made amends directly in a variety of situations. Often, they feel a sense of freedom after following through and making amends with someone—even just one person. It's not just a biblical concept; it also makes sound sense emotionally.

Step 10–12: A Review of the First Nine Steps

Once we've worked through the first nine steps, the three that remain are an expansion of the first nine. The first of these remaining steps extends our willingness to continue to take inventory and to make it a way of life. Step 10 says, *We continued to take personal inventory, and when we were wrong, promptly admitted it.* Self-knowledge is meant to be an ongoing process that we never stop. We should always be learning about who we are and what we are not. Eventually, something becomes clearer and more specific:

as we continue to take inventory and make amends when needed, we are developing a lifestyle of honesty. We are learning to be honest with others and ourselves.

This step adds a description of what the change in us will look like. With our willingness to check on our behavior continually, we are now able to *readily* admit when we are wrong. This is never easy, but it is an indicator of how honest we have been in our inventory.

Step 11 calls for us to be diligent in our relationship with God. It's a restatement of the first three steps, and it says, *We sought through prayer and meditation to improve our conscious contact with God, praying only for knowledge of His will for us and the power to carry it out.* To say that the 12 Steps are a spiritual guide for discipleship seems to be obvious with this step. We are called on to pray and to study God's Word. Many of those who live by the principles of the 12 Steps have developed the daily practice of having quiet time with the Lord as they pray, read the scriptures, and sit silently to hear what God wants to say to them.

Meditation on the scriptures has been a practice of Christians in recovery for many years. When Christians meditate, it is called "discursive mediation," which means its focus is not on emptying the mind but on Scripture. It involves reading a passage slowly and then sitting quietly to listen to God's voice in response to what you've read. Psalm 119:11 describes it: "I have hidden your word in my heart that I might not sin against you" (NIV). Luke 2:19 explains what it means to hide God's Word in our hearts: after Mary hears what the shepherds tell her about the baby Jesus, it says, "Mary kept all these things in her heart and thought about them often."

We are listening for God's will for us so that we can have the power to live in the center of His will. That's the point—we are to *do* God's will, not our own. For most of us, God's will gets all mixed with our own will and desires. When this happens, we should go back to the first principle we learned, which is that we are powerless. If we truly want to turn our wills and our lives over to the care of God, we seek to do so through obedience, by carrying out His will in our lives. That's also how we discover the power to carry out His will—we seek to obey the God who loves us.

Step 12 reviews the third commitment—our concern for others. It says, *Having had a spiritual awakening as a result of these steps, we tried to carry this message to others and to practice these principles in all our affairs.* Notice that the first thing this step affirms is that through working these steps, we have had a spiritual awakening. The steps are based on the Bible and are designed to lead us to experience this. But this doesn't mean "spiritual" in the way some people use the word—as an abstraction, a synonym for simply being sensitive. The spiritual awakening here is an awakening that is focused on God and on seeking to do what God wants us to do.

There's a reason this is the last step. Often, when people start working the steps, they get excited about what's happening within them. They want to help others get started, not realizing they've only just begun the process.

For example, Brian was doing well in his thirty-day treatment program. Then Melissa came in to the program, and Brian was smitten. He started spending time with Melissa, explaining the program and the steps to her. But they became an "item," and in spite of the cautions expressed to him by the staff, when they got out of the treatment program, they started dating. Their recovery was soon forgotten, and when Melissa broke off the relationship, Brian relapsed.

He was fortunate to be able to get back into the treatment program, and this time he listened when they explained that you can't stop working on yourself and switch to working on someone else's program. In order for him to stay sober, he had to work his program with a singular focus—Brian's sobriety and recovery. He hadn't understood what was meant by the phrase "working on the wrong side of the street." Melissa's recovery for Brian was the wrong side of the street. He needed to work on his side of the street!

When Brian started working on the wrong side of the street, he may have been motivated by a subconscious desire to avoid the difficult foundational work that only God could do. He needed to stabilize the changes in himself before trying to help someone else. This is a program for personal growth and change, and we need to impart what God *has done* for us, not what God *is going* to do for us. Think of it as the kind of evangelism where we share what we have experienced from God with others, not what we are hoping to experience.

I believe recovery is a synonym for what the Bible calls "discipleship." That's why I believe the 12 Steps are for everyone. We all have our addictions—or what some people call "our favorite sins"—that we continue to struggle with. That means we can all benefit from living out the principles of the 12 Steps.

Do the 12 Steps Work?

There have been a number of attempts to discredit the effectiveness of the 12 Steps, especially since it involves God and a spiritual awakening. Attempts to create a secular counterpart have typically failed. For years, there wasn't any formal research done, due mostly to AA insisting on the anonymity of those active in recovery. But with the growth of treatment centers, a broad research base has become readily available. Joseph Nowinski has collected most of the current research in his book *If You Work It, It Works!*,[6] where he reviews a large number of studies based on those who have been through a formal treatment program.

The studies were reviewed to see if there were any common factors that demonstrated that the 12 Steps worked and how the process worked. They wanted to see if they could identify any common factors that had led to treatment success. A large number of studies focused on relapse prevention. They basically asked, "How long did the person going through treatment stay clean and sober?" Four factors were identified, each related to how the steps are used.

First, they found that a person who went to four meetings a week for the first year was more successful than a person who went to three meetings or fewer per week—those who went to three meetings or fewer were more likely to relapse.

Second, they found that whether the recovering person got connected to what AA calls a "sponsor" was significant. A sponsor is a supportive person who guides the recovering person to work and

6   Joseph Nowinski, *If You Work It, It Works!* (Center City, MN: Hazelden, 2015).

understand the 12 Steps. A sponsor gives you automatic account-ability: this is the person you call when you are struggling with using or drinking again—struggling with relapsing.

The third factor is interesting: success was significantly higher when the recovering person was helpful to others—in other words, actively doing such simple things as helping set up the chairs for the meeting or cleaning up after. Those who were able to begin to break free from the typical self-absorption of the addict/alcoholic before recovery and become thoughtful of and helpful to others were more likely to be successful in their sobriety.

The fourth factor is highly significant, and it would have made Dr. Bob and Bill W. happy. They found that success in maintain-ing sobriety in recovery was directly related to the development of a personal relationship with God. In spite of the controversies surrounding the emphasis on God in the 12 Steps, those who take God seriously and develop a conscious awareness of God in their lives are more successful in staying sober than those who don't. Perhaps that's part of why secular attempts to avoid the spirituality of the 12 Steps have never caught on. Dr. Bob's "surrender room" was a precursor to the research on this last point.

CHAPTER SIX

Why Recovery?

Our goal has been to get the addict/alcoholic clean and sober; let's imagine we've been successful. Our addict/alcoholic, along with the family, has been in treatment, and we are celebrating her new sobriety. But the process doesn't end here. Hopefully, there's more to come, and it's called "recovery." We say "hopefully" because there is a term used to describe someone who just stops drinking and doesn't continue beyond this point: a "dry drunk." The alcoholic (or addict) is "dry" but hasn't changed. And the family of the dry drunk continues to live as if she is still drinking (or using). To get healthy, both the addict/alcoholic and the family need to work toward recovery.

If the addict simply stops using or the alcoholic simply stops drinking, he and his family suffer from a lack of behavioral change. The addict/alcoholic retains the old habit patterns along with the physical cravings, which, ironically, leads to a continuing struggle with the addiction/alcoholism. They call that kind of sobriety "white-knuckling it." That's because the chemical is still the focus of attention, meaning the addictive behavior continues as if they were still drinking or using.

Sandy told me about her husband's struggle. She said she had prayed for years that he would stop drinking. When he suddenly announced he was through with alcohol, she was ecstatic. That was ten years ago. But then she added, "I can't believe I'm going to say this, but there are many times when I wish he was still drinking. As crazy as that sounds, I would at least have something to blame for his behavior." She went on to explain that nothing in his behavior had changed—as far as she was concerned, he was just like he was when he was drinking. She had stopped going to Al-Anon, and when I suggested she go back, she agreed. She was living with a dry drunk who had resisted even the suggestion to start recovery. And in her frustration, she had given up on her own recovery.

The family will quickly recognize the behaviors of a dry drunk. She is just as impatient, resentful, angry, and judgmental as she was while actively drinking or using, and she overreacts to difficult situations just as she used to. Most of all, since she is rigidly white-knuckling it, she is really only one drink away from falling back into her old addiction. That's why she needs to get into recovery. She needs to recover all that was lost during her addiction.

That's also why the family members need to be in recovery. When living with a dry drunk, the family will quickly revert to expressing the same behavioral patterns as when the alcoholic was actively drinking. Nothing has changed, but we *can* change.

Let's say that someone started drinking excessively or using drugs at age fourteen. When a person becomes dependent on a chemical, things change in his brain, and he stops developing emotionally, spiritually, intellectually, and socially. Now let's say that our alcoholic/addict got into a treatment program and actively stopped drinking or using at age thirty-four. Emotionally, socially, spiritually, and even mentally, he is still at the same maturity level that he had reached when he started his addiction—in many ways, he is still fourteen. He needs to mature and fill in the years he lost. That process of learning new skills for living life is part of what is called "recovery."

Ron and Jenny's daughter started using drugs at age sixteen. At age twenty-three, she started to become sober but relapsed three or four times before finally getting on track. Jenny said she was like a sixteen-year-old. She had a sixteen-year-old's view of boy-girl relationships. She didn't know how to really look for a job. She was angry at God for not doing what she had told Him to do. She needed to work the 12 Steps and mature. That's the purpose of recovery.

In recovery, we also build character. When someone is addicted/ alcoholic, her strength of character begins to disappear. She loses integrity, she is always forced to live a lie, and the whole issue of having character becomes questionable. The addict/alcoholic doesn't deal reputably with others, and even her sense of morality is often compromised. While the addict/alcoholic may have had character in the past, it doesn't take very long for the addiction to destroy it.

The loss of good character can be summed up as the loss of integrity In the Psalms, David tells us about the importance of integrity. In Psalm 25:21, he writes, "May integrity and honesty protect me, for I put my hope in you." In Psalm 26:9 and 11, he adds, "Don't let me suffer the fate of sinners"— he could just as easily have said, "the fate of addicts/alcoholics"—and then he continues, "I am not like that; I live with integrity." And Psalm 119:1 says, "Joyful are people of integrity, who follow the instructions of the Lord."

Another aspect of strong character is being able to show other people respect and being worthy of the respect of others. The dictionary defines *character* as the moral and mental qualities distinctive to an individual. Abraham Lincoln once said, "Perhaps a man's character was like a tree, and his reputation like its shadow; the shadow is what we think of it; the tree is the real thing."[7] He is saying that what we think of a person is based on the shadow cast by her real character.

Working the 12 Steps in our recovery rebuilds our character, especially Steps 4–7, where we are sent on a journey to know ourselves. The truth is, if we *only* stop the additive behavior, we do not recover our character. We still cast the shadow of an addict/alcoholic. A recovery program is there to help the shadow begin to *reflect* good character.

Some Guidelines for the Addict/Alcoholic

What else do the addict/alcoholic and his family members need to pay attention to during recovery? First, everyone needs to slow down. Remember, Rome wasn't built in a day, and recovery doesn't happen overnight—it really takes a lifetime. So everyone must resist the temptation to try to solve every problem at once. Two important skills the recovering person will develop rather quickly will be patience and the ability to delay gratification—both of which are absent in the life of the active addict/alcoholic. The sponsor of a young man in recovery who I worked with advised him not to make any changes in his life for at least a year. That

---

7   Don E. Fehrenbacher and Virginia Fehrenbacher, eds., *Recollected Words of Abraham Lincoln* (Stanford, CA: Stanford University Press, 1996), 43.

meant he shouldn't change jobs, move, or date. His focus should be solely on his recovery. His sponsor knew that making changes too soon could be unsettling; it could cause anxiety and even lead to drinking or using again.

Mark was on a natural high when he became sober. He went to meetings every day—some were general or secular meetings, others were faith-based meetings. He was the most enthusiastic person there. He was full of questions. Two of the other meeting-goers were quietly starting to avoid him. Finally, someone whom he asked to be his sponsor was honest with him and counseled him about the urgency of his recovery. As his sponsor got him to slow down and begin to work on the steps, Mark began to see that his fear of relapse had created an artificial high of anxiety within him. That conversation he had with his sponsor was life-changing.

Second, we will need a new set of friends. We need to break off the toxic relationships of our past. If we go back to those relationships, it won't be long until we go back to our old toxic behaviors. That's part of why an inpatient or outpatient treatment program is essential—it's an opportunity to make new friends who have the same goals we have. Ninety meetings in ninety days will also provide a chance to create new friends. We can't afford to create a vacuum; we need support, and the people we drank or used with are not going to be supportive of our sobriety. At some point, we may reach a point where we can be around a few of our old drinking friends, but we can't push the river—we need to take our time on this.

Third, a major part of recovery is learning how to manage the emotions we have been avoiding for years. Up to the point where we stopped drinking or using, we were able to rationalize or deny what we were feeling, especially our painful feelings. Our best defense was to project the blame for those emotions onto our families or someone else. Or more frequently, we just numbed and suppressed the pain.

Now we can't numb ourselves anymore, and we must begin to face our pain and our shame. We may feel overwhelmed by it, but we need to bring those feelings into our relationships. One of the hardest to deal with will be all the resentments we have built up over the years.

We learn to face these emotions by working through the 12 Steps. Our fear of confronting them, especially our resentments, is one of the things we will overcome while working the 12 Steps.

Recovery helps us let down our defenses. This is accomplished as we hear other people's stories and share our own stories. As the pain emerges, one of the first things we must learn is how to identify what it is that we are feeling. We need to give it a name. Here's a list of some of the feeling words associated with the four primary negative emotions; it can help us identify and name what we feel. The intensity of the emotion lessens as you go down the list.

Anger	Fear	Sadness	Shame
Furious	Terrified	Depressed	Sorrowful
Enraged	Scared	Lonely	Worthless
Irate	Petrified	Hurt	Disgraceful
Seething	Panicky	Hopeless	Mortified
Upset	Apprehensive	Somber	Apologetic
Frustrated	Frightened	Distressed	Unworthy

(continued)

Anger	Fear	Sadness	Shame
Annoyed	Nervous	Moody	Embarrassed
Irritated	Timid	Blue	Regretful
Touchy	Anxious	Disappointed	Uncomfort-able

As a part of learning to identify our feelings, we must also learn to accept what we feel, that our emotions just *are*. There are no "right" emotions, just as there are no "wrong" emotions. We think of anger, fear, sadness, and shame as the primary negative emotions, but they are neither right nor wrong—they simply are. The "rightness" or "wrongness" of any feeling or emotion is found in what we do because of the emotion—how we manage the emotion. So first we should identify it and accept the fact that we are feeling it. As we learn to identify and accept our emotions, we will next learn how to manage them and how to talk about what we are feeling.[8]

Our emotions are what make us human. We are made in the image of an emotional God, who experiences anger and sadness (but not fear or shame—there is no fear or shame in God; after all, He is God). He also experiences the positive emotion of joy. He is able to feel joy because He is open to His other emotions.

One of the things we will discover in our recovery is that there are positive emotions and feelings that we never really experienced before. That's because what we do with one emotion affects all our emotions. When we repress painful feelings and emotions, we

---

8   For an expansion on these ideas, see Dr. David Stoop and Dr. Jan Stoop's book *SMART Love* (Ada, MI: Revell, 2017).

eventually repress all our feelings and emotions. We're left with only the out-of-control emotions of anger, fear, and shame.

The Family in Recovery

One of the saddest things that happens when the addict/alcoholic gets sober is that the family begins to break up. More couples divorce after the addict/alcoholic goes into recovery. It highlights the myth that if only the addict/alcoholic would stop drinking or using, the issues in the family would disappear. The truth is, the problems may even get worse at the beginning, and that is why the family must get into recovery along with the addict/alcoholic.

Unless everyone in the family gets involved in recovery, family members will still act out their old roles. They continue to be the heroes, the enablers, the lost children, the scapegoats, and the comics—only now, the roles don't seem to be necessary. Now they are free to feel the anger and hurt they repressed before, and they also live in fear that the addict/alcoholic will drink or use again. So they continue to walk on eggshells and panic if any old behavior patterns reoccur in the addict/alcoholic. Family members each need to enter recovery when the sober addict/alcoholic does. In fact, it would really be best if the family members were in recovery *before* the intervention. That way, they can prepare in advance for what it takes for a family that has been operating as part of the sickness to get healthier.

Here are some important tasks for the family in recovery. First, continue to use your support system. Be sure to work the 12-Step program of Al-Anon or Alateen. You need to work the steps for your own benefit. Get your own commitment to Jesus Christ settled, making Him your higher power. Then, as you take inventory, you will be able to identify the consequences of the role you played in the family disease. Each member of the family needs to understand her role and the roles of the other family members, and the family should talk together about how each family member is going to break free from her rigid role and be different.

Often, now that things are changing, the members of the family can allow themselves to feel the anger and experience the resentments they have accumulated over the years. However, this isn't the time to "let it all hang out." We need to learn how to appropriately express our hurts and anger carefully because we are not out of the woods yet. If some family members find it is necessary, opportunities to vent may be created within the treatment program or under its guidance.

Second, family members need to learn how to communicate with each other directly. One of the characteristics of an addictive/alcoholic family is that no one does this. The family members are all experts at circular communication—that is, instead of talking directly to the person they have an issue with, they talk to others and hope that they will resolve the problem. Healthy families engage in clear and direct communication with each other. If I have a problem with you, I talk directly to you; I don't bring in someone else to carry the message.

When the addict/alcoholic was active in his addiction, words were a way to either attack in anger or get defensive. Now the family members must learn the principle of "speaking the truth in love" (Eph. 4:15 NIV). That means when anyone speaks the truth, no one will judge him for what he says. You as a family may need help with this, so finding a counselor who understands the family dynamics of addictions and who will work with the whole family together may be helpful.

Third, it's time to move forward into the future rather than linger in the past. The past must at some point be surrendered to God (Step 3). This doesn't mean we gloss over the pain of the past in order to protect the recovering addict/alcoholic. For either the addict/alcoholic or her family members, surrendering the past requires that everyone has been communicating honestly and openly. Most treatment programs that have a family week will help your family deal with some of the painful parts of the past.

We release the past through forgiveness. Forgiveness cancels the unpayable debt of the past. We decide that we are going to forgive—that's our goal. We may not feel like forgiving, but that's okay, for we are only making the commitment that we *will* forgive.

Once we decide that we are going to forgive, we enter a process where we grieve the losses of the past. Grieving requires the feelings of anger as a protest and sadness as a sign of resignation. We've probably already encountered that anger and protest over what we have lost as a family and as individuals. Perhaps now is when we are actually able to face the sadness of the losses and grieve and accept the reality of what has been lost. When we have experienced both, we are ready to forgive what is owed to us—that which can never be repaid—just as God does when He releases the pain of our past sins through forgiveness. All we can do about what's been lost is grieve—and then finalize everything by canceling the debt that is owed but unpayable through forgiveness.

We are the beneficiaries of our forgiveness. Sometimes, one of the addict/alcoholic's family members is so hurt and angry about the past that he refuses to forgive. Give him time to understand that forgiving doesn't do anything to change the past, nor does it do anything to change the one who has hurt you; its benefits are always and only for the forgiver. For it to benefit the one who has been forgiven, that person must enter into a reconciliation process with the forgiver.

Dr. Anderson Spickard, in his book *Dying for a Drink*, points out that the family needs to be in recovery whether the addict/alcoholic is or not. He writes, "The process of surrender includes releasing the alcoholic to God's care and detaching themselves from his ups and downs. For most people, the key to this detachment is the acceptance of the disease model of addiction … It is only when they begin to see the alcoholic as a sick person in need of help that they find the spiritual and emotional resource they need for their own recovery."[9]

What about Relapse?

Family members need to be involved in their own recovery regardless of what the addict/alcoholic does. But don't be surprised if the one you love relapses and it feels like déjà vu. You have been here before, but you also haven't been *here* before. I was talking with a nurse in a treatment center and asked her what it was like for someone to relapse and come back into treatment. She replied, "At

---

9   Anderson Spickard and Barbara R. Thompson, *Dying for a Drink: What You Should Know about Alcoholism* (Waco, TX: Word Books, 1985), 107.

first, it made it seem like it was hopeless, at least for that person. But then I found that even though they had been through the program before, all was not lost. The second time they came in, they were different than they were the first time. They had made progress; they had just relapsed."

Even though most recovery programs do extensive education to prepare the person for how to avoid relapse, recovering alcoholics and addicts do sometimes relapse. It may be soon after they leave treatment, or it may be years later. It's not inevitable, but when it happens, it is discouraging. And you as the family can't let up. If the person doesn't get right up and back on track, you may need to have another intervention. But you can't just accept it and say, "I knew it was going to happen." It doesn't have to happen, but it can happen.

Education about avoiding relapse can be as simple as a warning: don't get too tired, too bored, or too hungry. Typically, those who relapse become a little too self-confident. They feel like they have it all handled, and so they may get back together with old drinking buddies or cut back on attending meetings, or they might not keep up work on their inventories (Step 10) or their relationships with God (Step 11).

The Serenity Prayer

The goal of recovery is to experience serenity. That's why, at every meeting, you hear people reciting the Serenity Prayer together. But how do we define *serenity*? The *Oxford English Dictionary* defines it as "the state of being calm, peaceful, and untroubled" and gives an example of how the word can be used: "an oasis of serenity amidst the bustling city."

There are three important words in the first part of the prayer, and they help us define serenity. The words are *acceptance*, *courage*, and *wisdom*. If you've been to meetings, you probably have already memorized the first stanza, which says, "God, grant me the serenity to *accept* the things I cannot change, *courage* to change the things I can, and *wisdom* to know the difference."

The acceptance of those things in life that cannot be changed is the beginning. Those things include our past, our childhood issues, the mistakes we have made, and the consequences of those mistakes. We all have a tendency to want to rehash the past in order to make it something other than what it was. Serenity begins with acceptance of what was and will always be.

But some things can be changed, and it will take courage to face what can be and must be changed. Taking inventory of our pasts and making amends with others requires courage. Relationships can be changed, but only in the here and now. There is truth to the reality that today is the only day in which we can exercise the courage to bring about change.

The hard part is having enough wisdom to know what can be changed and what cannot be changed. One would think that would be an easy task, but what is "easy" is ruminating over our pasts and ignoring our present opportunities for change. James 1:5 tells us, "If you need wisdom, ask our generous God, and he will give it to you. He will not rebuke you for asking." God Himself is the source of all wisdom, and He willingly gives us wisdom when needed.

We need to remember that we direct the prayer for serenity toward God. It is a gift of life recovery. God is the source of our serenity, as Proverbs 3:5–6 reminds us: "Trust in the LORD with all your heart; do not depend on your own understanding. Seek his will in all you do, and he will show you which path to take."

The serenity prayer you recite in recovery meetings is only part of the whole prayer. Here it is in full:

God, grant me the serenity
to accept the things I cannot change,
courage to change the things I can,
and wisdom to know the difference.

Living one day at a time,
enjoying one moment at a time,
accepting hardships as the pathway to peace,
taking, as Jesus did, this sinful world
as it is, not as I would have it.

Trusting that God will make all things right
if I surrender to his will,
so that I may be reasonably happy in this life
and supremely happy with him forever
in the next.
Amen.

You can see other principles of recovery in the rest of the prayer: "living one day at a time" and "accepting hardships as a pathway to peace." Words like *trusting* and *surrender* are also key elements of healing and wholeness. Remember, recovery, as a Christian experience, is really discipleship. When someone you love is addicted, the healing and recovery calls everyone in the family to be involved and to be wise disciples of Jesus.

NEWLIFE

Help in Life's Hardest Places

Talking about the things no one else will, to bring healing to those who've lost hope

"**I have been living with my secrets** for 30 plus years while failing time and again to stop and all the while them getting worse. For the first time I have learned more about why it is happening, developing an action plan to change, and creating a network of support."

— Jack
Intensive Workshop attendee

When you or someone you love is in crisis, you need a trusted friend to walk alongside you—a helper who's been there and understands, but who also has the training and skill to offer practical help.

New Life Ministries, founded by Steve Arterburn, exists to go into life's hardest places with you.

For over 30 years, we've provided expert answers to people just like you on our call-in radio show, *New Life Live!* We also offer a host of other resources, Intensive Workshops, and referrals to a carefully selected network of counselors.

Visit NewLife.com today to see how we can help, or call 800-HELP-4-ME. We want to hear from you!

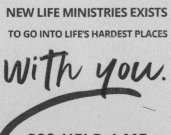

NEW LIFE MINISTRIES EXISTS
TO GO INTO LIFE'S HARDEST PLACES

with you.

800-HELP-4-ME
NewLife.com

About New Life Ministries

New Life Ministries, founded by Stephen Arterburn, began in 1988 as New Life Treatment Centers. New Life's nationally broadcast radio program, *New Life Live!*, began in early 1995. The Women of Faith conferences, also founded by Stephen Arterburn, began in 1996. New Life's Counselor Network was formed in 2000, and TV.NewLife.com, the ministry's Internet-based television channel, was launched in 2014. New Life continues to develop and expand their programs and resources to help meet the changing needs of their callers and listeners.

Today, New Life Ministries is a nationally recognized, faith-based broadcasting and counseling nonprofit organization that provides ministry through radio, TV, their counseling network, workshops, and support groups, as well as through their numerous print, audio, and video resources. All New Life resources are based on God's truth and help those who are hurting find and build connections and experience life transformation.

The *New Life Live!* radio program, still the centerpiece of the ministry, is broadcast on Christian radio stations in more than 150 markets. It can also be seen on several network and online channels.

New Life's mission is to reach out compassionately to those seeking emotional and spiritual health and healing for God's glory. New Life Ministries Resource Center receives thousands of calls each month from those looking for help.

For more information, visit newlife.com.

About Stephen Arterburn

Stephen Arterburn, M.Ed., is the founder and chairman of New Life Ministries and host of the number-one nationally syndicated Christian counseling talk show *New Life Live!*, heard and watched by more than two million people each week on nearly two hundred stations nationwide. He is also the host of New Life TV, a web-based channel dedicated to transforming lives through God's truth, and he also serves as a teaching pastor in Indianapolis, Indiana.

Stephen is an internationally recognized public speaker and has been featured on national media venues such as *Oprah, Inside Edition, Good Morning America, CNN Live*, and *ABC World News Tonight*; in the *New York Times, USA Today, US News and World Report*; and even in *GQ* and *Rolling Stone* magazines. Stephen has spoken at major events for the National Center for Fathering, American Association of Christian Counselors, Promise Keepers Canada, the Lifewell Conference in Australia, and the Salvation Army, to name a few.

He is the bestselling author of books such as *Every Man's Battle* and *Healing Is a Choice*. With more than eight million books in print, Stephen has been writing about God's transformational truth since 1984. His ministry focuses on identifying and compassionately responding to the needs of those seeking healing and restoration through God's truth. Along with Dr. Dave Stoop, he edited and produced the number-one-bestselling *Life Recovery Bible*.

Stephen has degrees from Baylor University and the University of North Texas, as well as two honorary doctorates, and is currently completing his doctoral studies in Christian counseling. He resides with his family in Fishers, Indiana.

Stephen Arterburn can be contacted directly at SArterburn @newlife.com.

About David Stoop

David Stoop, Ph.D., is a licensed clinical psychologist and family counselor in the state of California. He has worked with families and marriages for more than thirty-five years. Dr. Stoop is also an ordained minister, holding a master's degree in theology from Fuller Theological Seminary and a doctorate from the University of Southern California.

Dr. Stoop is frequently heard as a cohost on the nationally syndicated *New Life Live!* radio program and television show. In addition to being the founder and director of the Center for Family Therapy in Newport Beach, California, he serves on the executive board of the American Association of Christian Counselors.

At Fuller Theological Seminary, Dr. Stoop is an adjunct professor who teaches courses associated with family therapy. Through his counseling, he has helped thousands of people around the country understand addictions of many sorts and learn how to love someone well in the midst of this gripping disease.

An award-winning author of more than thirty books, Dr. Stoop is also the coeditor of the *Life Recovery Bible*, which has sold well over a million copies.

Dr. Stoop and his wife, Jan, have been married for more than fifty years. They live in Newport Beach, California, and have three sons and six grandchildren. Together, he and Jan have led seminars and retreats all over the United States as well as in several other countries.

At David C Cook, we equip the local church around the corner and around the globe to make disciples. Come see how we are working together—go to **www.davidccook.com**. Thank you!

transforming lives together